THE SLOPEMASTS
A HISTORY OF THE
LOCHFYNE SKIFFS

THE SLOPEMASTS

A HISTORY OF THE
LOCHFYNE SKIFFS

MIKE SMYLIE

First published 2008

The History Press
The Mill, Brimscombe Port
Stroud, Gloucestershire, GL5 2QG
www.thehistorypress.co.uk

British Library Cataloguing in Publication Data.
A catalogue record for this book is available from the British Library.

ISBN 978 0 7524 4774 2

Typesetting and origination by The History Press
Printed in Great Britain

Contents

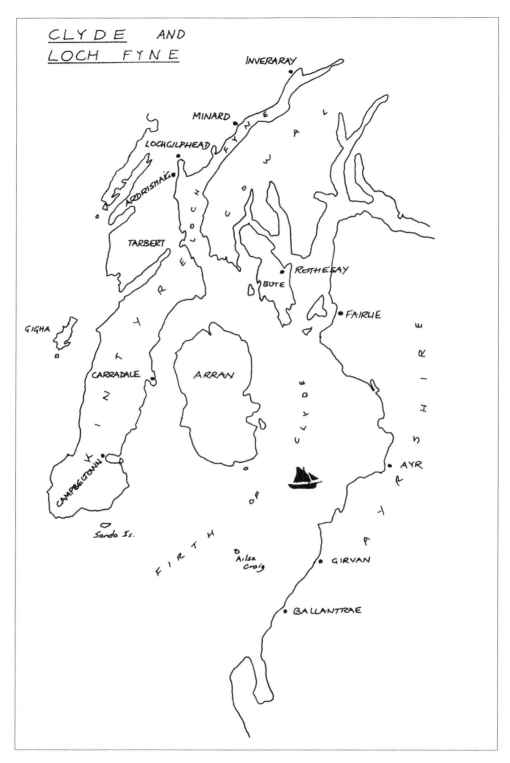

Map of the River Clyde and Loch Fyne.

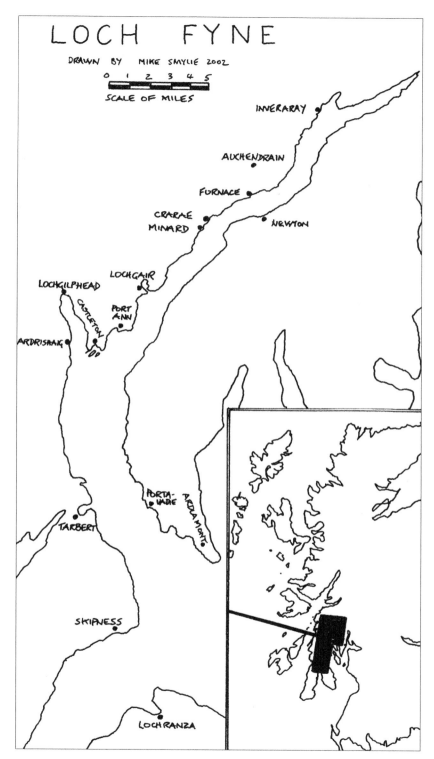

Map of Loch Fyne, illustrating places mentioned in the text.

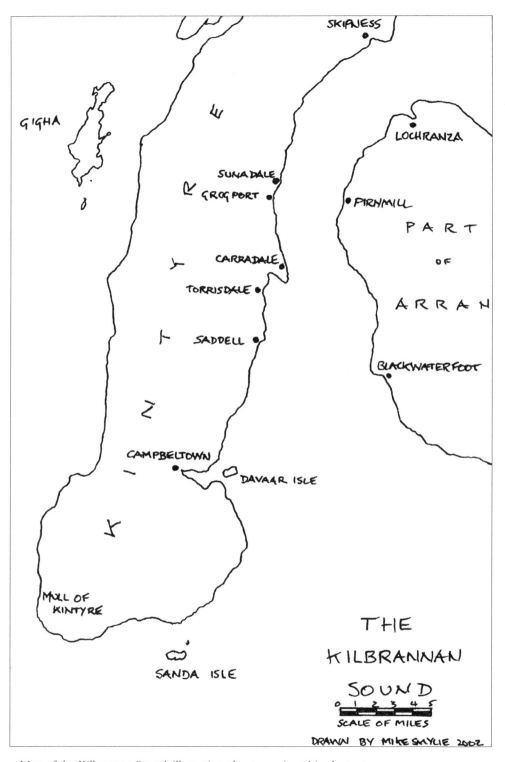

Map of the Kilbrannan Sound, illustrating places mentioned in the text.

Preface

It is now over twelve years since I sold my Lochfyne skiff, *Perseverance*, which was subsequently sunk off the coast of Portugal. I think I can honestly say I've never regretted anything so much as the day I parted from her company. She was a truly beautiful boat, history oozing out of each worked piece of timber that had gone into her original structure, the scent of the fishermen's toil being almost as powerful as the smell of diesel from the Kelvin J4 engine, their strength being matched by the power in the rig. During the period that I owned her I learnt so much about the skiffs, the ways of the fishermen and their fishing techniques. However, I am fully aware that I probably only scratched the surface. I was fortunate to meet Angus Martin of Campbeltown, author of *The Ring-Net Fishermen*, who not only directed me along the proper avenues and became a friend, but also introduced me to the family of Archie Mathieson, the original owner and skipper of the boat. His daughters, Kate MacWilliam and Mary Smith, were finally re-introduced to the boat one windy autumn day at Crinan in 1991, exactly forty-five years after their father had sold her due to his retirement from the fishing industry. The following year they, their brother Alex, and many others, helped celebrate the eightieth anniversary of the day *Perseverance* was launched in Campbeltown. Thus I met many people who knew the boat, some indeed who had worked upon it. To Mary and Kate it had been their life-line during years of great hardship. I quote from one of the many letters I received from both Mary and Kate, this one from the latter dated October 1991:

> Although I was present at the launching I do not remember the occasion as I was only three years old but I know it was a proud day for my father who had worked hard and saved to fulfil his ambition of owning his own boat. He lost both his parents as a very young man so the effort was all his own – it is easy to understand his choice of name. She was his pride and joy and was cared for as such …
> You see she was not just a boat to us, she was our life support and that she did proudly.

Sadly Mary has since passed away so will be unable to read this.

I dedicate this book to the memory of Archie Mathieson and his family, and the hundreds of ring-net fishermen who sailed Lochfyne skiffs. I believe that they were true fishermen, hunters of the sea, who, unlike many of today's fishermen, had a real understanding of the job they did and its impact upon the planet. As is often said, the world is a poorer place for their passing.

Thanks are due to Robert Prescott, Angus Martin, Neil Short, Kate MacWilliam, Lachie Patterson and The Scottish Fisheries Museum, as well as all those who have contributed through various snippets of information and helped produce the bigger picture.

Introduction

Over many hundreds of years Britain has had a huge diversity of working boats operating around her coasts. These, from the maritime perspective, are generally contained in what is termed the 'vernacular zone'. Each particular area or region has had its own types of vernacular craft that were employed in a variety of maritime occupations such as coastal trade, fishing, pilotage, salvage, life-saving and many more. Although it is difficult to specify borders between each area because of the cross-flow of influences from area to area, there are definite distinctive types of craft for ethnologists to concentrate their researches upon.

However, when researching vessels in the vernacular zone, there are many more problems than there are when researching, for example, naval vessels. Vernacular craft are usually, by their very nature, low-tech products suited for a particular job and often relatively anonymous in their design. They are mostly fashioned from the experience of their operators, built by the eye of the builder and worked arduously so that they often have a short working life. Thus surviving designs and drawings are, on the whole, non-existent, as are any archival sources outlining their evolution.

Fishing craft probably have the widest diversity of any of these working craft. Fishing is an occupation carried out in every part of the coast, whereas undertakings such as pilotage and salvage very often only occur where major ports or seaways are nearby. The coastal trade, although affecting all parts of the coastline up to the beginning of the twentieth century, usually involved vessels of a similar design that plied routes from one side of the country to another.

Small coastal fishing boats, on the other hand, often never worked outside of their locality and thus tended to remain in their specific area. It was only after the 1830s that fishermen began to sail further afield in their quest for fish, and in doing so developed their craft into larger boats.

Studies of Scottish fishing craft have mainly concentrated on the East Coast and the Northern Isles. On the West Coast, the variety and history of fishing craft has generally been neglected, whilst that which has been written has largely tended to relate their designs to those of the East Coast. Yet the West Coast has its own peculiarities that have led to altogether different boats developing through their usage. Amongst these West Coast craft is the Lochfyne skiff, which emerged from several generations of innovation as one of the prettiest workboats to have graced the British shores.

Although neither extraordinary in design nor pioneering in boat technology, the Lochfyne skiff was the last evolutionary stage in the era of sailing boats in the Clyde area, prior to the advent of motorisation in the first decades of the twentieth century. Furthermore, the design was unique in that it was developed specifically for ring-net fishing – a different, more aggressive way of fishing that had come into use around Tarbert in the 1830s and which, within a century, had become generally accepted by Scottish fishermen. In several parts of the country, however, its use was always regarded with suspicion and even hostility by some.

As a generalisation, a Lochfyne skiff was a half-decked vessel, in excess of 25ft in the keel length, of a relatively light construction, rigged with one standing lugsail and, usually, a jib set on a bowsprit. The stem was upright, the sternpost was raked – although not as acutely as that of the zulu – and the keel sloped to give a shallow forefoot and deep heel. Such a hull shape gave excellent manoeuvrability in confined waters. Its forward-stepped mast raked considerably.

The proximity of the Loch Fyne herring fishery to the markets of Glasgow gave the fishery the impetus it needed for growth in the nineteenth century. Late in the previous century John Knox had observed that the diet of the working people in Glasgow, who earned no more than 8s a week, was potatoes and herring. Although the setting down of railway routes throughout the nineteenth century never contributed to these expanding markets to any extent – the nearest station being at Tarbet, close to the head of Loch Long – the advent of steam did. The fish curers chartered steamers, usually drifters from the East Coast, as did the Argyll and Bute Fishermen's Association later on, and these carried the fresh fish direct from the fleets, mainly to Glasgow.

The face of Britain changed rapidly in the nineteenth century with the advance of the Industrial Revolution, yet for the fishing fleets change was slow. Some benefits were obvious in that machine-made cotton nets replaced the older hemp nets, capstans aided the hauling of the drift-net on the larger boats and steamers worked off the East Coast. But in the more inaccessible reaches of Scotland these innovations were hardly noticed. Except for the introduction of the ring-net, the use of which, to begin with, hardly constituted a technological advance and the transportation of the fish by steamer as mentioned, this was the case in Loch Fyne. Fishing progressed throughout the majority of the century in much the same way as it had for generations past.

It was against this background that the Lochfyne skiff appeared in the Campbeltown fleet for the first time in 1882. It was a vessel with an entirely different capability in that the fishermen could live aboard with some degree of comfort whilst 'at the fishing', and one designed specifically for the mode of fishing practised by the majority of the fishermen. Norton, in his *The End of the Voyage*, describes her thus:

The Loch Fyne skiff or nabbie is a graceful bird-like craft as seaworthy and as handy as any vessel of her size. She rarely exceeds 35ft. in length and even the larger boats are virtually open, being built with a deck forward for one-third of their length only, with beneath it a sort of cabin shelter. She has a curved stem, bold sheer, and a very characteristic stern, pointed, with a raked and curving stern post and beautiful buoyant lines, at the quarters. She draws plenty of water aft, and the keel slopes up steeply towards the stem. The whole hull, particularly the stern, have a look strongly reminiscent of Norwegian craft. The influence of Norway may be seen in many boats on the east coasts of the British Isles and we shall meet it again later, but it is curious that this western boat should carry the stamp of her ancestry more clearly then do some of her sisters, the luggers of the eastern shores. Another attractive feature of this hull is that many, instead of being painted, are clear varnished which gives them a very light and clean appearance.

There are two points worthy of a mention here. Firstly there seems to be confusion between a skiff and a nabbie, the latter being the fishing boat of the east side of the Firth of Clyde. Nabbies were slightly different to the skiffs in that they had fuller sterns and a more raking mast, a few setting a mizzen also. Nabbies were also described as being 'of about 25 by 8 feet, entirely open; they have a very broad, round stern, and narrow bow, rigged with one large lug-sail and jib; they are handsome, and work and sail well'. We shall consider them in more detail later. The great American naval architect Howard Chapelle made the same mistake. When discussing the various sources of available plans of British fishing boats, he says of the Lochfyne skiff *De Wet*, 'this is a nabbie, and is an able type of fishing boat'. A nabbie it certainly was not.

The second point is Norton's reference to a Norwegian ancestry. Other writers such as Edgar March have made similar suggestions. However, one of the intentions when I started my research into these vessels was to critically explore and evaluate the claim that the Lochfyne skiffs evolved primarily from East Coast influence. Different influences from several quarters were brought to bear upon the fishermen and boatbuilders alike that resulted in the unique shape of the skiffs, so that there are other possible precursors to these boats. Thus I found possible influences coming from Cornwall, France and indeed as far off as Spain, and a wide range of other factors that potentially contributed to the origins of the Lochfyne skiffs.

One other error has crept into today's archives that should be mentioned and that characterises the previous lack of research into the Lochfyne skiffs. Laird Clowes, when detailing the summer 1936 Special Exhibition of British Fishing Boats (that such an exhibition was assembled shows the high esteem in which fishing was then regarded and one simply cannot imagine any public body repeating the exercise today) labelled one such example as 'a Loch Fyne Scaffie'. His description reads, 'The stem is curved like that of a "scaffie", but she is considerably deeper aft and also the upper part of the stern is flared out so as to produce something very similar to a counter, although this does not project beyond the raking sternpost'. Since a counter stern, by its very construction, is a projection outboard of the sternpost and because the Lochfyne skiff clearly has a straight or almost straight sternpost with no projection, one wonders which Lochfyne skiff he was attempting to describe! Furthermore, the stem, although slightly curved, is not curved like that of a scaffie and the forefoot is not as rounded.

To explore the different possible roots of the design of the Lochfyne skiff I found that documentary evidence was forthcoming because of the abundance of government publications concerning fishing, such as the Registers of Sea Fishing Boats, Fishery Board Reports and Parliamentary Papers relating to fishing. In addition, a wide variety of travellers published their observations from journeys around western Scotland from the late eighteenth century onwards. Furthermore, the statistical accounts for Scotland provide information on individual parishes in the 1790s and 1840s.

Early pictorial evidence mostly came from the William Daniell aquatints although other sources are available that indicate a general idea of vessels in use in the eighteenth and nineteenth centuries. For the skiffs themselves, the best source of photographs is the McFee collection, now at the National Maritime Museum at Greenwich. However, due to high reproduction costs imposed by the Museum, we are unable to use these pictures in this publication.

Through studying the available iconography, a clear picture of these skiffs emerges, showing how changes in attitudes to fishing, and an increasing knowledge of boat technology, were accompanied by subtle changes in hull form and rig. This has been particularly useful in attempting to identify the Irish Sea wherries, which in the past have been regarded as misnomers in the maritime field.

The following chapters form a progressive argument displaying how boat design evolved in the area under consideration, identifying the craft in use, which, it is hoped, will lead to a greater understanding of the roots of the Lochfyne skiff. In addition, several examples of skiffs are discussed, as are the motorised ringers that superseded the skiffs in the third and fourth decades of the twentieth century.

All photographs are from the author's collection, unless otherwise credited. Whilst every effort has been made to determine the ownership of photographs, mistakes might occur, for which the author apologises.

one

The Scottish Herring Fisheries up to 1845

Fishing in Loch Fyne

The arm of the Kintyre and Knapdale peninsular juts southwards for some 60 miles from its junction with the rest of Scotland along a line, following roughly the route of the Crinan Canal between Lochgilphead on Loch Fyne, and Crinan at its western end. Loch Fyne itself, the longest of all the Scottish lochs, runs between Skipness Point in Kintyre and Ardlamont Point at the southern tip of Cowal, right up to Clachan, 37 miles distant. The upper part of the loch starts at Otter Spit and throughout its length is no more than 2 miles wide at the most. Below Otter Spit it is between 2 and 4 miles wide, the broadest stretch being at its junction with the short Loch Gilp.

There are a number of sheltered harbours or bays where small craft can either lie alongside a pier or run up the beach. On the west side these are at Skipness, Tarbert, Ardrishaig, Lochgilphead, Castleton, Port Ann, Lochgair, Minard, Crarae, Furnace and Inveraray. Seldom today will a fishing craft be seen in any of these except Tarbert, and occasionally Ardrishaig, when traversing through the Crinan Canal. Lesser fishing hamlets once existed at Auchendrain, Lower Goatfield, Sandhole, Drynlia, Cumlodden, Inverae, Auchgoyl, Shirdream and Newton, the latter being on the east side of the loch.

The harbour of Inveraray, perhaps the oldest of these having had a quay since at least 1709, was once called 'Slochk Ichopper', literally 'the gullet where vessels bought or bartered fish'. The importance attached to the herring fishery is reflected in the town's coat of arms that depicts a net with a herring and the motto *Semper tibi pendeat halec* (may there always be herring in your net). Probably because of the proximity of the ancestral home of the Dukes of Argyll, it was a popular stopping-off point on the itinerary of numerous travellers touring Scotland during the latter part of the eighteenth and early nineteenth centuries. Their descriptions of the town, and especially the fisheries, have enabled a picture to be drawn up of the boats in use. The vast majority of these travellers mentioned the state and quality of the herring in Loch Fyne.

More than 300 years before the first of these travellers arrived, Scottish historian Hector Boece reported in 1537 that there 'is mair plente of herring than in any seas of Albion'. Two decades later, in 1555, the Scots Parliament found that the fishermen from the western side of the Clyde had 'resortit to the fisching of Loch Fune and uthers Lochis in the North Ilis for the making of hering and uthers fischeis'. Another twenty years later Bishop Leslie wrote, 'In the Westir Seyes … the hail haruest and behinning of Winter is a gret schule of herring, bot in na place sa fatt and of sa pleisand a taste as in that loch mair Westirlie, quhilke afor we expremed vnder the name

'Loch Fine' by Robert Wallis, from a print of unknown source.

of [Loch] Fine'. Then, in 1603, Sir Walter Raleigh spoke of the Dutch selling herrings valued at £1½ million, employing 20,000 Scots, and all the herring coming from the Scottish West Coast, most notably Loch Fyne. Centuries before this, though, in 836, Netherlanders supposedly came to Loch Fyne to purchase salted herring. The suggestion is that it was the Loch Fyners who taught the Netherlanders to cure herring and hence were largely responsible for the later Dutch dominance, but this is a tenuous claim and has to be regarded with some suspicion.

Around 1630, according to a 'Memorandum concerning the fishing along the coast of England, Cornwall, etc.', there were 800 'slaying boats of between five and six tons each' fishing between 1 July and 25 October and that, at its peak, it was possible for there to be 1,500 boats as well as '200 Cowper boats about 12 Tun apiece' that bought the herring and transported it to markets. The writer also noted 6,000 fishermen employed on the West Coast, presumably in a part-time capacity during the herring season.

Daniel Defoe, travelling in the early eighteenth century, found a land devoid of harbours and ports suitable for shipping but saw 'Fishing-Barks and Boats, which are in the Season employ'd for the catching of Herrings, of which the Shoals that are found on this Coast in the Season are incredible, especially in the Clyde, in Loch-Fine, and about the Isle of Arran, which lies at the Mouth of the Clyde'.[1]

As already mentioned, a stream of travellers came to Inveraray, one of the first being Thomas Pennant in the early 1770s. He found almost 600 fishing boats fishing for the huge shoals, the peak of the fishery being between September and Christmas. The drift-nets they were using were 100 fathoms long, set at a depth judged to be where the shoals were. He observed that often one boat would have a successful catch whilst another, adjacent to it, didn't catch a single fish, and thus the fishermen perpetually enquired amongst themselves as to the depth at which the nets were set.

In 1784 B. Faujas de St Fond described Inveraray as the capital of Argyllshire but not as a town, thus denoting its smallness.[2] He suggested that in France it would be termed a village, but a pleasantly situated one 'upon the side of beautiful Loch Fyne'. He also noted that larger vessels had an abundance of herring, yielding considerable revenue to the country, recognition perhaps that they were being exported.

One of the most influential visitors was retired Edinburgh bookseller John Knox, who was invited to make an official tour of the Highlands for the government, keen to extend the herring fisheries. Knox ultimately wrote three discourses and made a whole host of observations and suggestions, some of which were adopted by the British Fisheries Society that set up four fishing stations in Scotland at the close of the eighteenth century – at Tobermory on Mull, Ullapool, Lochbay on Skye and, later, Pultneytown in Wick. Of Loch Fyne, he said it 'enjoys every possible advantage for the fishermen ... situated amongst the shoals of herring', and that the fishermen, upon sighting the shoals, would immediately be out in their boats in whatever weather to 'sink their nets'.[3]

Thomas Newte also noted that 'this arm of the sea produces herrings in great abundance ... five hundred boats are employed in the proper season for the fishing'[4] and 'take a considerable amount of herrings; part of which are salted for the use of the neighbouring country, and part sent to Glasgow'. The minister for Saddell and Skipness, in the Old Statistical Account, described the Loch Fyne herring as being 'of a richer and more delicate taste than those caught in the Western Isles, or the Coast of Ireland'. In the same account, the Revd Fraser from Inveraray stated that the loch 'has been from time immemorial noted for its herrings'. In fact many of the travellers share this opinion of quality. Peter Anson added that some 900 boats followed the fish and that most of the catch was sold to France and Spain.

John Stoddart, travelling to these parts in 1799, found that the herring were bigger and of a finer flavour than those on the East Coast, and that they constituted the diet of both the rich and poor alike.[5] The former ate them for breakfast whilst the poor lived almost exclusively on them, served with potatoes. Such habits were to last for well over one hundred years.

Fishing Outside of Loch Fyne

A Roman, Polinus, reported that the people of the Western Isles lived on fish and milk. That was in AD 240. In 1630 some 120 boats were catching codling at the mouth of the Clyde, and two years later Charles I decreed that only native fishermen should fish in the waters enclosed by a line between the Mulls of Kintyre and Galloway.

The Firth had no shortage of fishing bases, from Campbeltown and Carradale, on the eastern side of Kintyre, through the Isles of Bute and up towards Greenock and Glasgow, and down the eastern side of the Clyde to Stranraer and Portpatrick which, although outside of the Clyde, lies within the limits defined by the Charles I decree. Furthermore the Isle of Arran had stations at Blackwaterfoot, Pirnmill, Lochranza and Lamlash, where, in about 1695, Martin found a harbour with good fishing of cod and whiting. He also noted that 'barks and boats' were in use at a harbour close to a castle at the head of Loch Kenistil, presumably Lochranza.

Rothesay, on the Isle of Bute, had eighty fishing boats fishing for herring in about 1695. By 1763 this had decreased to thirty boats which appear to have been fishing busses – the large

Inveraray wherries from the 1804 *Scotiae Depicta* by J. Fetler, plate XVIII.

herring boats used for deep-sea fishing for the bounty payments that had been introduced in 1750.

The Kilbrannan Sound that is situated between Kintyre and Arran is deep, like Loch Fyne and was also regarded as being rich in herring. Thus fishing boats operated from Skipness, Grogport, Carradale, Torrisdale, Saddell and Campbeltown. The herrings were said to be of a similar, superior quality to those from Loch Fyne and on an evening, 200–300 boats could be seen fishing at the close of the eighteenth century. At about the same time, the building of harbours at Carradale, Skipness and Sunadale (by Grogport) were suggested to accommodate vessels upwards of 15–30 tons to carry fish to the 'red herring houses in Liverpool'.

Loch Long was also noted for its shoals that frequented the loch and afforded employment to a number of fishermen. Loch Goil had a substantial fishery, albeit inferior in quality to those of Loch Fyne. At Dunoon 'herrings frequent the loch at times'. In Greenock, during the time of Charles II, the society of Herring Fishers had particular privileges and they cured herring in an enclosed area called the Royal Close. To Defoe, the town was the chief herring port of the whole of the West Coast and he observed that the Glasgow merchants employed Greenock ships to catch the fish and transport the catch to market, hence leading to their overall control of the whole fishery.

Some fishermen from the Moray Firth kept their craft on the Clyde and travelled over from the East Coast each summer to participate in the annual herring fishery, landing at Glasgow,

Paisley and Greenock. They returned home with 'pocket fulls of money' and built themselves fine houses on the firth.

On the eastern side of the Clyde the principal herring stations were established at Ayr, Girvan, Ballantrae and Stranraer, and Portpatrick, as already mentioned. Stranraer, at the head of Loch Ryan, was once the centre of a flourishing herring fishery, although this had declined by the late eighteenth century. Large quantities of 'deals, plank, large timbers, and iron' were imported, mostly from Norway, Gothenburg and the Baltic, presumably for boatbuilding; R. Pococke, during his third tour in 1760, noted that the inhabitants 'live chiefly by the Herring fishery, and use boats built of deal, which last five or six years'.

In 1817, William Daniell said that the people of Galloway 'do not starve, though they do not fish, build ships, trade abroad …'. Of Portpatrick he said it 'has nothing in it to invite our stay, it's a mean dirty homely place'. Defoe had thought them stupid eighty years before! Things must have improved soon afterwards, fishing-wise, for by 1821 there were twenty boats employing one hundred men, with 120 boats in the harbour during the herring season. Outside of that season they caught cod for which they became renowned.

Outside of the Clyde, the herring fishery thrived, albeit intermittently. Lochs Craignish and Crinan had some £500-worth of herring caught over a five-week period by twenty to thirty boats in 1785. Loch Melfort briefly had visits from the huge shoals. Tobermory fishermen went out in their open boats and caught herring for their families and sold the surplus to their neighbours. Lack of salt, due to the oppressive Salt Laws, prevented the development of an industry and was one reason why the newly-built British Fisheries Society village failed in its objectives.

Further north, herring were caught annually in Loch Duich and Glenelg, the latter being visited by busses from the Firth of Clyde. Nearby, Loch Hourn became an important fishing centre with curing huts being set up on its northern shore, the remains of which can still be seen. On Loch Carron, after a remarkable fishery in 1791, the children of the parish went and collected 'lapfuls of herring' which their families ate, only to become ill:

> their blood was vitiated. When they were let blood in the fever, it had an appearance, when it congealed, of the blood of a boiled pudding, or of an ugly kind of jelly. Their breath smelled strong of fish. In proportion as they fed, soberly or voraciously, on the herring, the fever was more or less severe. Such as lived mostly on fish, and other strong food, suffered dreadful agony. The poor people, that lived upon water-gruel, suffered very little.

Herring fishing thrived for a while at Ullapool, and curing stations were built around the locality. Likewise, the Outer Hebrides, especially Castle Bay and Stornoway, became centres of successful fishing. One of the most descriptive and apt passages of writing concerning the herring fishery is of Lochranza by John McCulloch in 1824:[6]

> The whole bay formed a beautiful sight when I first saw it, on a fine evening in August, when it happened to be the rendezvous of the herring fleet. The busses that were purchasing fish, were at anchor in the loch, each with its flag flying, and surrounded by boats in groups delivering their cargoes, while some were running alongside, and others hoisting their sails to stand out again to sea. The dark festoons of the nets hanging over the sides, the white topsails above displayed to dry and

the bright yellow hulls of the herring boats, with all their variety of brown and yellow and white sails, and with the smooth green sea below, reflecting every tint, formed combinations of colouring even more exquisite than those produced by the elegant forms of these boats, with their tall masts and pyramidal sails, dispersed and contrasted and grouped in every possible manner. Far away towards the Argyllshire coast, the sea was covered with a swarm of boats of all sizes and kinds, with sails of all shapes and colours, standing away towards Loch Fyne on every possible tack, and gradually diminishing to the sight till they vanished under the distant land. The shore was another scene of life which served to complete the picture. Other boats drawn up on the beach, or ranged along the margin of the water, were delivering cargoes to the country people and to the coopers; the whole green beneath the castle being strewn with fish, and nets, and casks, while horses, and carts, and groups of people in motion, with the hum of their voices, and the hollow sound from the coopering of the casks re-echoing from hill to hill, added to the smokes of numerous fires employed in the cookery or in boiling the oil, rendered the whole scene of confusion, activity and bustle, contrasting strangely with the wild solitude of the mountains around, and the calm repose of the setting sun.

Notes

1. *A Tour through the whole Island of Great Britain* (London, 1927).
2. *A Journey through England and Scotland to the Hebrides in 1784* (Glasgow, 1907).
3. See: *A view of the British Empire, more especially Scotland, with some proposals for the Improvement of that country, the extension of the fisheries and the relief of the People* (London, 1784); *Observations on the Northern Fisheries with a Discourse on the Expendiency of Establishing Fishing Stations or Small Towns in the Highlands of Scotland and the Hebride Islands* (London, 1786); *A Tour through the Highlands of Scotland and the Hebride Islands in 1786* (London, 1787).
4. *A Tour in England and Scotland in 1785 by an English Gentleman* (London, 1788).
5. *Remarks on the local scenery and manners in Scotland during the years 1799 and 1800*, 2 vols (London, 1801).
6. *The Highlands and Western Isles of Scotland*, 3 vols (London, 1824).

two

The Drift-net and Line Boats

McCulloch's fine description, other than providing a picture of a typical fish-curing station of the time, gives us an important clue as to the type of vessel these fishermen used. He states quite clearly that the boats had bright yellow hulls, by which we presume he means that they were made from natural wood, and coated in oil for protection. He provides another clue by describing the sails as being pyramidal, thus suggesting the boats had lugsails. Other evidence from two decades after McCulloch's depiction in the 1820s, points to a change in boat type about this time. Before we study this new type of boat that, I believe, led to the development of the Lochfyne skiff, we must first document the fishing wherries that were the common vessel around the loch and surrounding waters.

When bounties were introduced in 1750 to encourage the growth of the herring fishery, fishing for herring was mostly being undertaken in small open boats, some 16ft in length and crewed by four or five men. Owned primarily by individuals, they were generally only used during the herring season and lay dormant at other times, apart from the being used occasionally to carry the odd sheep or to travel about in inaccessible parts of the coast. The average coastal dweller on the West Coast had a small plot of land to cultivate or intermittent work on a local estate or quarry, and the herring fishery simply served as a way of stocking up food for the long, dark winters ahead.

Knox, in 1785, assumed that from early times the fishermen had been using 'little open wherries or boats, such as the Highlanders generally use at the present day'. He estimated there were 1,600 of these Highland wherries in the Firth of Clyde, each crewed by four men. The following year, however, he noted that the Highland boats had four oars and six or seven crew and that the West Coast fishermen were 'navigating the main ocean with boats not much larger than a London sculler, and many of them, called Norway skiffs, about that size … the Highland boats are nearly of one size, slender built and but indifferently equipped'. These vessels were, presumably, those he saw in the Hebrides, as it is known that small double-ended craft were brought over from Norway to Shetland, Orkney, the Outer Hebrides, Northern Ireland and probably other parts of the West Coast. He wasn't impressed by them even if, as he noted, there were 2,000 in use in the West Highlands and Hebrides. 'To go up the Sound of Mull, even in the most favourable season, was a dangerous experiment for a small open boat, such as Oban afforded.'

It is evident that these boats or *batas* – Gaelic for 'small boats' – did evolve from a traditional Scandinavian design. The clinker-built, double-ended shape with wide planks, such as that in use in Northern Europe, is widely accepted as having derived from the Viking ships of the Norse era (although there is an argument that several centuries earlier the boats of the Saxon invaders were similar in shape and construction). Brought over to Shetland and Orkney, at first due to a lack of timber, as whole boats and then piece-meal to be assembled by local boatbuilders, the success of the shape was soon accepted. Before long local influences brought about small regional differences as seen in the boats of, for example, Shetland today. By the eighteenth century they were being carried as far as Northern Ireland where they developed into the drontheim; the earliest picture of one is in a painting of Portstewart in 1822.[7] Like Shetland and Orkney, and Northern Ireland, much of the West Coast had a shortage of boatbuilding timber, thus similar boats were initially imported and then built locally, and the *bata* was, generally, a localised development of those that were imported.

According to the local rector of the Glassary parish in the Old Statistical Account of the 1790s, Ardrishaig had '30 boats annually employed by the small tenantry living upon Lochfine side in the herring-fishery; each boat requires 4 hands … there are 3 boat-carpenters'. It appears the village grew quickly from having only a few fishing boats to being a thriving place with 'regularly laid out streets, in which one house seems to march forward, while its neighbour makes a retrograde courtsey – its cheerful harbour, filled with the wealth of fishermen, the herring boats – the stillness prevails, alone broken by the plash of oars, or the harsh guttural Gaelic of the rowers …'. Much of its wealth came from the Crinan Canal and the frequent steamer connection to Glasgow, not the fishing. It is easy to forget, however, that the herring fishery wasn't the only fishery; outside of the herring season many folk went to the line fishery which was within the confines of the loch. Wherries were suitable for this. According to James Anderson in the 1780s, the fishermen regarded wherry-rigged vessels as being the only proper ones for lining, but he went on to suggest that the same vessels could be used for herring fishing after the Dutch method.[8] This suggests he didn't visit Loch Fyne and only saw the so-called Norway skiffs in use further up the West Coast.

Inveraray often had 500 boats fishing in the season. Confirmation of this number comes from the Revd Paul Fraser in the OSA, who also noted that each boat is crewed by four men on average. Most of the men had come from outside the so-called town where only eight fishermen lived. Thomas Garnett, arriving there at the turn of the nineteenth century, estimated the number of craft to be between 500 and 600.[9] He added that 'the groups of these little fishing vessels, with their circling nets, make a beautiful moving picture … each boat is covered with a kind of sail-cloth, to form a covering for the four men who compose the crew'. Garnett also observed that at night the fishing boats formed a line across the loch and that, during the day, the fishermen gutted herring, slept and sang 'Celtic tales to the sound of the bag-pipe'. Pennant described the 'chearfull noise of bagpipe and dance [that] echoes on board' the 'some hundreds of boats in a manner [that] covered the surface of Loch Fyne'.[10] Garnett's boats, then, lie low in the water, with hardly any sheer and without much shape. Others, such as Stoddart and Bowman, noted the sail-cloth covering used as shelter for the crew, thus suggesting that the crew slept aboard their boats.

In the parish of Saddell and Skipness, the minister recorded thirty wherries, 6–10 tons with two crew, for carrying the herring to market and sixty rowboats, four men to a boat, and that 'both are sometimes promiscuously employed' for fishing. At Kilfinan, on the east side of the loch, there were twenty-one open boats each manned with four hands and constantly employed in the catching of herring in Loch Fyne, East Kintyre, Arran, Clyde, Loch Long and further. The farmers relied upon the fishery to pay their rent, although in the south of the parish the Revd Alexander McFarlane wrote of their 'drinking proving to their having carried on a ruinous contraband trade with the Isle of Man'. Thus smuggling and fishing are mentioned as joint occupations.

Loch Long from *Observations on a Tour through the Highlands of Scotland* by T. Garnett, vol. I, p181.

The connection with the Isle of Man allows a comparison of types of craft to be made, and a probable assumption of what is meant by a wherry. In the past the term 'wherry' has been used with a customary lack of precision, and it thus demands a more thorough critique to clarify its definition. In the Isle of Man, a wherry was described as a light boat with a fore-and-aft rig which was in use there up to the 1830s when the dandy rig was introduced.

There appear to be two distinct sizes of wherry – a larger vessel of about 18 tons which was used to transport smuggled goods around the Irish Sea, and a smaller version of about 6 tons, used to ferry goods ashore at secret locations, away from the prying eyes of the revenue officers. That larger wherries were used for smuggling is undisputed: in 1765 there was seen, according to the Collector of Customs at Liverpool, 'a wherry at anchor and a great many horses and casks upon the shore … the casks carried back to the wherry in yoals … the wherry weighed anchor and went to sea'. The same collector wrote of one wherry that had been captured, 'She is a fair boat about 16 or 17 tons loaden and sails comparatively well and carries 10 or 12 men always armed'. The speed of the wherries was the chief reason for their use in this business.

Evidence for the smaller wherries is more forthcoming and the dimensions of one boat are given. Of boats condemned in 1778, after fishermen were arrested for smuggling, there were 'small boats that none were decked … boat number 11 measuring 19 feet 12 inches and 8 feet 2 inches in breadth is computed in the said certificate at seven and one fourth tonnes though by his computation it should only be seven tonnes'. In contrast, the large wherry *Heads of Ayr* is 52 tons. In 1777, fifteen wherries were said to measure 82 tons in total, calculating to 5½ tons each.

Although there is no evidence of these wherries fishing in Manx waters – the two-masted wherries were used by the merchants for buying fish directly off the fishermen – there is evidence that they fished in Scottish waters. The 1785 First Report from the Committee appointed to enquire into the state of the British fisheries noted that wherries were employed in the fishery during the greatest part of the year. In Saltcoats, as well as there being six or eight vessels that went to the North Highland herring fishery, there were a considerable number of wherries going to the fishery in Loch Fyne and the Kilbrannan Sound, according to the New Statistical Account of 1845.

Between 1742 and 1847 fishing wherries operated from Lamlash, in Arran. Irish wherries sailed to fish in Shetland in 1756. Wherries, amongst other types of craft, were reported fishing in Loch Broom in 1798 and were about 2 tons. Much later, in 1883, the yachtsman Robert Buchanan described an Arran wherry as:

> now nearly extinct, is a wretched-looking thing without a bowsprit, but with two strong masts. Across the foremast is a bulkhead, and there is a small locker room for blankets and bread. In the open space between bulkhead and locker birch-tops are thickly strewn for a bed, and for a covering there is a huge woollen waterproof blanket ready to be stretched out. Close to the mast lies a huge stone and thereon a stove … rude and ill-found as these boats are, they face weather before which any ordinary yachtsman would quail.

This substantiates the claim that the fishermen slept aboard during the fishing season. Unfortunately, however, the size of this wherry was not documented.

On the east side of Loch Fyne, at Kilfinan, there were 111 fishing wherries belonging to the parish, each of them being crewed by three men and costing about £40–50. Thus the general consensus is that a wherry is a small transom-sterned or double-ended vessel with two masts, probably with a schooner rig – otherwise termed the wherry rig. Photographic evidence for such a craft in Loch Fyne comes from several sources. J.Fetlar's print in *Scotiae Depictae* of 1799 entitled 'The Port of Inveraray' shows a wherry-rigged vessel sailing inward, the hull having hardly any sheer, as depicted by Garnett. The bow is bluff while the stern seems quite sharp. An undated engraving by Robert Wallis entitled 'Loch Fine' shows two Norway-type skiffs from which two crew members of each are setting drift-nets. It has been suggested that this view was taken at the upper part of the loch and that the castle on the left is at Dunderave Point, north of Inveraray. The large schooner-rigged vessel is probably a fish carrier while the square-sterned, bluff-bowed vessel could be either. Nets are drying on the shore and several small craft can be seen in the distance.

In his journal entitled *A Voyage round Great Britain 1814–1825*, William Daniell shows several excellent aquatints of wherries, including a superb view of a transom-sterned wherry entering Maryport harbour in what is now Cumbria. Another view is of Ailsa Craig, probably taken near Girvan. On the beach are seven small double-ended open craft of which six have masts that are raked backwards; the one in the foreground has a sail lying over its gunwale. These six display, for the first time, vessels with typically raked masts, probably sporting lugsails, for which

Double-ended Ayrshire skiffs, from *A Voyage Round Great Britain* by W. Daniell vol. III, 1818.

Wherry sailing into Maryport, Cumberland. From *A Voyage Round Great Britain* by W. Daniell.

Loch Fyne and the Clyde later became renowned, and supported by evidence documented in the NSA, from the parish of Glassary, that the boats became larger a few years before 1845, and that the lugsail was introduced by the Ayrshire fishermen. In the minister's own words, 'their boats are becoming larger and better; and the Ayrshire fishermen have brought in a good style of skiff, with a single lug-sail. A few years ago they were all wherry or schooner-rigged'. The same improvement in size and quality of vessels was noted for the parish of Saddell and Skipness. It appears that the Ayrshire fishermen first came to Loch Fyne to collect bait for their lines and subsequently settled in Ardrishaig. Thus it seems pretty certain that, at some time, probably in the 1830s, the wherry rig, set on both transom-sterned wherry-types similar to those in and around the Isle of Man and the double-ended Norway-type craft, was superseded by the lug rig that the Ayrshire men introduced. There is a further inference that these Ayrshire men were persuaded in the advantages of the lug rig by fishermen who were descended from a colony of fishermen from Pitsligo, near Fraserburgh. However, it is just as possible that they were convinced after seeing the French boats that came to fish and trade in the Clyde, for they, too, set a lug rig, sometimes in double-ended craft. Probably the exact reasons for this conversion to the lug rig will never be known, but the fact that it was a dramatic change is indisputable.

There is one more development in the herring fishing pattern that added to the general consensus amongst some fishermen of the need for a superior type of boat. With the introduction of the ring-net at Tarbert in the 1830s, a boat with a greater ability for manoeuvrability was required, at first to evade detection after the practise was outlawed, and later to fish closer to the shore. In turn a new type of fishing craft was to prove crucial in the development of the ring-net fishery.

Notes

7. See: MacPholin, D., *The Drontheim – Forgotten Sailing Boat of the North Irish Coast* (Dublin, 1999).
8. *An account of the present state of the Hebrides and Western Coasts of Scotland* (Edinburgh, 1785).
9. *Observations on a Tour through the Highlands of Scotland*, 2 vols (London, 1811).
10. *A Tour in Scotland* (London, 1774).

three

From Wherry to Skiff

The Introduction of the Ring-net

The evolution of the ring-net started with fishermen using drift-nets as seine-nets in one small boat off the beach, probably in 1833. In the next phase two boats (later referred to as 'neighbour boats') were used, so that the net was set out by one boat whilst the second boat held the other end fast. Once the net was so set it could then be trawled between the two boats before its ends were brought together and the hauling process begun. The history of the introduction of this method has been extensively researched by Angus Martin, and his resulting work, *The Ring-Net Fishermen* (Edinburgh, 1981), is considered to be one of the most comprehensive and sympathetic local studies of a regional fishery. It therefore needs no repetition bar what is necessary.

Between the 1830s and the banning of the practice of trawling a decade later, a change in boat design had become apparent. In 1848, in a letter criticizing the method, the writer refers to 'a class of boats, not owned by the regular fishers of herring, [which] have of late years had recourse to trawling of fish'. These, it is suggested, are the trawl skiffs which have double-ended hulls rigged with a single lugsail.

The earliest description of such a vessel comes from the Washington Report of 1849, which was produced after Captain John Washington, under instruction from the Admiralty, investigated the fishing vessels in the aftermath of a particularly bad gale which had devastated the fishing fleets of the East Coast of Scotland the previous year. In it we find various descriptions of fishing vessels in use all around the British coast, and the two replies to his queries from informants in Ardrishaig and Port Glasgow are also important.[11]

To begin with, John Wood of Port Glasgow tells us this:

… we have no fishing boats here, but in Gourock or Largs there are some good specimens of the boats used in Loch Fyne, &c. They are by no means handsome, but are very stiff under sail, and Weatherly; their form is spoiled, I think, in order to get them with a short keel for working in narrow water, as well as for saving the cost of building, the price being reckoned by the length of the keel. They are open, and in these sheltered water lochs this is, perhaps, attended with no inconvenience, though in the open sea in a gale of wind boats above ten feet broad might very well carry a half-deck, with gangways, which would render them more safe than when quite open; the weight of the deck is perhaps the most serious objection; it would, no doubt, be also inconvenient in a crowded boat.

Class 1 of these boats, 27 feet over-all, and 11 feet breadth, is getting numerous, and is, I think, a decided improvement as compared with the old boats; the stern is upright, the bow

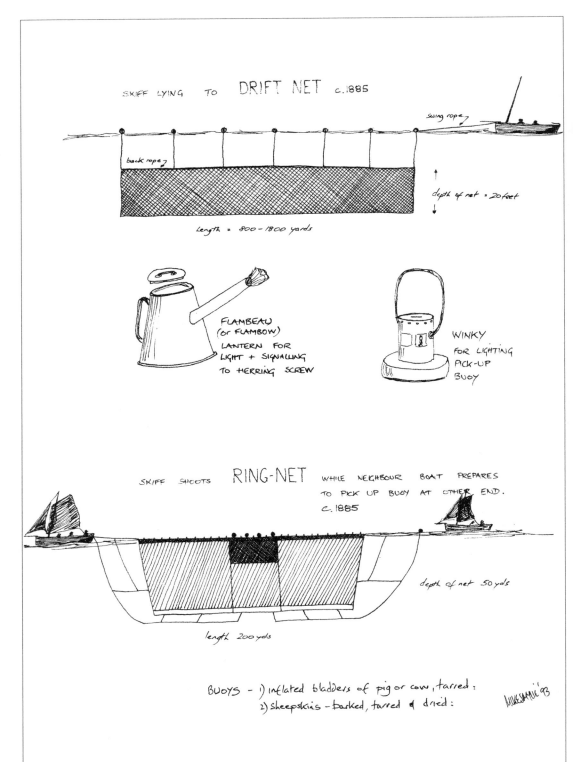

SKIFF LYING TO **DRIFT NET** c.1885

swing rope

back rope

depth of net = 20 feet

length = 800 - 1800 yards

FLAMBEAU
(or FLAMBOW)
LANTERN FOR
LIGHT + SIGNALLING
TO HERRING SCREW

WINKY
FOR LIGHTING
PICK-UP
BUOY

SKIFF SHOOTS **RING-NET** WHILE NEIGHBOUR BOAT PREPARES
TO PICK UP BUOY AT OTHER END.
c.1885

depth of net 50 yds

length 200 yds

BUOYS - 1) inflated bladders of pig or cow, tarred:
2) sheepskins - barked, tarred & dried:

ANGUSMARTIN '93

Right: Unknown painting of trawl skiff at Tarbert, pre–1884.

Below: Trawl skiffs and two smacks at Campbeltown New Quay, *c.*1890. (Photo courtesy of Angus Martin.)

narrow, resembling a yacht, and they sail fast by the wind. These boats, I am told, are for the most part built at Rothesay, Fairlie and Ardrishaig; many are also built in Greenock, Gourock, Campbeltown, and other places. Until late of years they were built entirely open, and rigged with two heavy gaff sails and jib; in fishing, they used to unship the mainmast, and work entirely with the foresail; by degrees the smack-rig has come wholly into use, as well as the half-deck. These boats make long voyages, with only two men; in fishing they have more. On the Ayrshire coast there is a numerous class of boats, about 25 by 8 feet, entirely open; they have a very broad, round stern, and narrow bow rigged with one large lug-sail and jib; they are handsome, and work and sail well.

No. 1 of the drawings I send is made from measurements taken from a new boat built at Rothesay, and comes very near the usual form of the Loch Fyne boats; they are, however, a good varied, principally in the midship section, some having much more of a hollow in the floor than others; they are all pinched for length of keel, because the price is constantly made at so much per foot keel.

No. 2 is an improved bow, introduced by Mr. Fyfe of Fairlie, and I have no doubt will get into general use, being better adapted to the cutter rig than the full bow, as the jib lifts the bow, while the after leech of the mainsail depresses the stern, whereas the schooner (or wherry rig as it was called) required a full harping and narrow stern, to keep the bow up under the weight of the foresail, the foremost being close forward, and upright.

Mr. Sutherland from Ardrishaig gives us the following facts in his letter dated 2 October 1849:

1. About one-fifth of the boats used in the fishery are open boats.
2. They are chiefly built at Fairlie, Rothesay, Tarbert, and Ardrishaig.
3. Northwards from Loch Crinan they are generally open; and southwards to the Mull of Galloway about one-fifth open. They average about four and a half tons burthen.
4. The half-deck is not considered any inconvenience; and the introduction of the deck in boats has been within the last 25 years.
5. The fishermen live on board the boats while engaged in the fishery; the half-deck affords them protection from the weather, a sleeping and cooking apartment.
6. They prefer lying afloat when the harbours will admit of it, particularly so on account of drying their nets aboard; the Loch Fyne boats do not take the ground easily, being sharply built.
7. They generally last from 15 to 20 years.
8. There are four classes of herring fishing boats in Loch Fyne. 1st Class – Length of keel 21 feet; half-decked. Rig – mainsail, jib and foresail; one mast. Cost of hull, sails, mast, and oars, &c., 60l. Complement of herring nets, fully mounted with buoys, buoy ropes, &c., 40l; total cost, 100l.

   2nd Class – Length of keel 19 feet; half-decked. Rig – mainsail, jib and foresail; one mast. Cost of hull, sails, mast and oars, &c., 50l. Complement of nets, mounted as above, 35l; total cost 85l.

   3rd Class – Length of keel 18 feet; one half of this class half-decked. Rig – mainsail and jib; one mast. Cost of hull, sails, mast and oars, &c., 39l. Complement of nets, mounted as above, 30l; total cost, 69l.

   4th Class – Length of keel 17 feet; all open. Rig – lug sail; one mast. Cost of hull, sail, mast and oars, &c., 20l. Complement of nets, mounted as above, 25l; total cost 45l.

Painting of Tarbert Harbour, Loch Fyne, by David Murray ARA, *c.*1870.

Clinker trawl skiffs at Tarbert, *c.*1880.

Half-decked smack and small line skiff, pictured at Blackwaterfoot, Arran.

Postcard of the pier, Brodick, Arran.

Inveraray harbour from an unknown postcard.

P.S. – The boats employed in Loch Fyne and its vicinity in 1848 were, at Inveraray and Lochgilphead, 1,1283; at Campbeltown and Islay, 546; at Rothesay, 219; at Greenock and Ayr, &c., 478; making a total of 2,526 boats, manned by 7,933 fishermen and boys.

From this information it is clear that the introduction of the smack for herring drifting had occurred in the 1820s, which agrees with Gray's assertion that half-deckers had arrived in Loch Fyne about this time.[12] It must be noted that, unfortunately, in all the copies of the Washington Report seen by the author, no copies of the drawings referred to by John Wood are included. However, what is clear is that the Ayrshire men were using 25ft double-enders, with rounded sterns, rigged with one lugsail. These became known as nabbies and were mostly used in the line fishery. Similarly, the Loch Fyne fishers had introduced the lug rig to their small boats which were probably being used for the ring-net fishery, while the drift-net fishers had rigged their wherries with gaffsails.

Several reasons might have persuaded the men in their abrupt adoption of the half-decker, as many of the smacks appear to have been. Firstly, as we've already seen, the practise of sleeping aboard was nothing new. Secondly, in 1824 the commissioners for the Herring Fishery had advised the allotting of sums of money towards the building of piers and for the repairing of boats belonging to the poor fishermen. Two years later the government had set aside £3,000 for this purpose, and numerous applications were submitted from those with wrecked boats or boats badly damaged by the weather. Grants not exceeding half the cost were paid to those who could prove hardship, and who had families to keep. By 1827 grants had been paid up to a maximum of £70, and Inveraray fishermen received £21 5s while at Rothesay the figure was £59, according to the Fishery Board Reports. Two years later grants of £300 were paid throughout Scotland during a year when fishing was poor because of adverse weather. The annual report noted that

A variety of boats from both the East and West Coasts of Scotland assembled in Loch Fyne for the herring season, *c*.1980.

'the boats, with few exceptions, were small in size, ill provided with fishing materials, seldom cleaned or furnished with floor-boards or pumps, and the fishermen rarely ventured in them above two or three miles'. Who could blame them! The third reason could have been the repeal of the dreaded Salt Laws which, in turn, invigorated the herring fishery as salt became more easily available for even the smallest communities to cure their fish.

Thus, by the time of the Washington Report, it is evident that the lug-rigged skiff of about 25ft in length and some 6ft in beam, had been adopted. According to Martin, a clinker-built version of this cost from £12 to £20 in 1852, which agrees with the price of £20, including sails, mast and oars suggested by Sutherland from Ardrishaig. Ten years later this had risen to £40.[13] Presumably the level of grant had increased by then, perhaps up to £10, providing some of the cost. These were open boats, light and swift, and as often as not, rowed, especially when avoiding detection. Martin also suggests that they were un-ballasted until ring-netting was legalised, when ballast was normally carried.

By 1850 it had become obvious that a distinct type of craft was being used for the ring-net operation. In a report by John Miller, the Fishery Board's general inspector, it was noted that between £500 and £600 had been paid to one Tarbert carpenter for trawl skiffs. In 1860, thirteen trawl skiffs, complete with nets on board, were seized by the crew of HMS *Jackal* in a raid upon Tarbert in the early hours of the morning of Sunday 23 September. The following year Peter McDougall, a young fisherman from Ardrishaig, was shot by marines while fishing aboard the trawl skiff *Weatherside*, neighbouring with another skiff, *Star*. These were generally propelled with oars, the lugsail not often being used and sometimes even left on shore. A few of the skiffs, such as the *Pelican* of Tarbert, had a jib, according to the fishing boat registers.

It is also clear that the drift-net fishers were using smacks, a number of which were launched in 1862, a year in which many Tarbert ring-net fishers gave up that method and reverted to

Lochfyne fishing boats by E.W.H. Holdsworth from *Deep-Sea Fishing and Fishing Boats*, p332.

drift-netting, after the authorities clamped down under the terms of the repressive legislation against trawling, which included the confiscation of smacks belonging to fish curers found to be buying trawled herring. By 1867, however, all the Acts against trawling were finally repealed, allowing the trawl fishery to compete against the traditional use of the drift-net.

During the 1870s the size of the trawl skiffs increased up to 30ft in overall length as demand to fish further afield grew and boatbuilding techniques improved. Some, it is suggested, had small spaces below short foredecks, although these were only big enough to stow a few stores. Many of the fishermen, when away from home and fishing in convoy, slept aboard a smack that was sailed alongside the fleet specifically for accommodation. Many of the older smacks had become redundant as, by this time, many of the drift-net fishers from the upper part of Loch Fyne, originally opponents of trawling, had begun participating in it as they recognised the advantages in the amount of fish caught and the reduced cost in furnishing themselves with a boat and gear. However, it wasn't long before these fishermen realised that a small increase in the size of their boat enabled a small forecastle to be incorporated.

Notes

11. See: *Report on the Loss of Life and Damage to Fishing Boats on the East Coast of Scotland* by J. Washington, 1849.
12. *The Fishing Industries of Scotland 1790–1914* (Oxford, 1978).
13. See: Mitchell, D., *Tarbert in Picture and Story* (Falkirk, 1908).

four

The Lochfyne Skiff

What is a Lochfyne Skiff?

Like the many other types of British fishing boats, the Lochfyne skiff is unique. For the sake of clarity, it can be described as a half-decked, double-ended fishing boat of a relatively light construction, the characteristic features of which are the sharply-raking and slightly curved sternpost, the long sloping keel equal to, or exceeding 25ft in length, and the upright, straight stem (although there sometimes is a slight curve) with shallow forefoot. The freeboard is relatively low to ameliorate the hauling process of the net. The rig, on a heavily raked mast, is the standing lug, usually with a foresail set on a bowsprit. Under the foredeck is a forecastle big enough for the fishermen to sleep in. Furthermore, according to the Registers of Sea Fishing Boats, the skiffs are regarded as being over 4 tons burthen and built after 1882.

It has already been mentioned that these skiffs have been confused with other, similar, boats in the past. The nabbies of the east side of the Clyde, the great-line boats of that coast, although having distinct similarities to the Lochfyne skiffs, have a much rounder stern and are not the same. Likewise, the great Edgar March, in his seminal *Sailing Drifters* (London, 1952), referred to the Lochfyne skiffs as zulu skiffs, something they definitely were not with many dissimilarities in hull shape. In the 1936 Special Exhibition of British Fishing Boats, Laird Clowes labelled one skiff as 'a Loch Fyne Scaffie', in deference to those boats of north-east Scotland. Again they are not scaffie-type craft, despite such a craft being in use many years before the Lochfyne skiffs. Likewise, the zulu design emerged in 1879. We have already discovered that the trawl skiffs were of a similar shape and had been around for over 40 years. However, it can be said that all three, with their certain similarities, did evolve through a Scandinavian ancestry with local influences (and in the case of the Lochfyne skiffs other possible long-distant influences) bearing upon their development. All fishing craft evolve not only through tradition, but from the mode of fishing, the type of harbour or beach they work off, as well as through individual requirements of the fishermen themselves. So impressed were the Manx fishermen with these Lochfyne skiffs that they developed a similar design – the Manx nobby – adapting it for their own locality, and thus displaying the effect of fishermen admiring the boats of other communities and adapting or copying what they've seen.

Skiff *Treasure* ashore at Minard, *c.*1930. (Photo courtesy of Willie Crawford.)

Skiff *Flying Fish* – built by J. Fyfe in 1907 – on regatta day.

Skiff at Ardridhaig – possibly *Meta*, built by J. Fyfe in 1892.

Lochfyne skiff *Fairy Brae* off Davinar Isle, Campbeltown, *c.*1890.

Builders of the Skiffs

On Boxing Day in 1883, Hugh Carmichael informed the Napier Commission that 'we have got them larger now; this year or two back some have been getting what they call decks and they can live on them now. We consider them quite large enough at twenty-four to twenty-six feet to be handled with oars to pull the trawl instead of sail'. He was, of course, referring to the type of vessel used for the ring-net; he added that drift-nets had almost been given up. The length he refers to is that of the keel.

The first two Lochfyne skiffs, as is generally accepted today and supported by Carmichael's evidence, were introduced into Campbeltown in the spring of 1882 by fisherman Edward McGeachy of Dalintober, Campbeltown. The two boats – *Alpha*, CN185, and *Beta*, CN186 – had been built in Girvan, possibly by Jas Kirkwood, and were immediately distinguishable from the trawl skiffs by the incorporation of the forecastle under the foredeck with sleeping platforms for four men, a stove for warmth and cooking and limited storage space. The days of lodging aboard smacks or camping ashore were finally over for those adopting the design.

Unfortunately there are no surviving records of these first two boats except for their entries in the Registers of Sea Fishing Boats. *Alpha* was sold to Ardrishaig where she was registered as 276AG, and then, about 1900, to Rothesay, after which nothing is known about her. *Beta's* registration was closed in 1895 after a short and reasonably successful career.

Although boats of the same design were quickly built – the *Betsy*, CN22, *Wild Deer*, CN81, *Selena*, CN91, *Chreagliath*, CN144, *Mairi Chanog*, CN157, *Mari Bhan*, CN205, *Nelly*, CN321, *McMillan*, CN341 and *Fairyfield*, CN316 all appearing the same year – others continued with the earlier skiff design. Some owners chose to adapt their present vessels by adding one or more strakes and fitting a small forecastle, leading to a dumpy kind of vessel referred to by the Ayrshire fishermen as the 'Penny Bank'.

Two years later a host of Lochfyne skiffs were being launched from builders in Girvan, Greenock, Gourock, Rothesay, Ardrishaig, Tarbert and Campbeltown. Within a few more years the list had grown considerably (see appendix for full list of Lochfyne skiff builders).

Far from simply being a slightly larger version of the earlier trawl skiffs, the new skiffs had several improvements built into the design over the first years of their introduction. Thus the sternpost raked at a more extreme angle and the keel had more drag, both increasing the efficiency of the hull when manoeuvring in confined waters relatively close to the shore, as ring-netting often necessitated. Different boatbuilders incorporated subtle modifications to suit their own ways of building, so two boats were seldom identical.

Much of the Campbeltown fleet originated from the town in those early formative years, with Lachie Lang being the principal boatbuilder. John Wardrop was listed as a boatbuilder in the 1891 census and he built the *Hartington*, CN396, in 1883. Likewise, the Tarbert and Ardrishaig fleets were produced by local builders. On the other hand, builders such as James Fyfe, who began building skiffs in 1882 – he built the aforementioned *Nelly* – also supplied vessels for the Loch Fyne and Campbeltown fleets. Fyfe, originally employed in the Fife of Fairlie boatyard, moved to Port Bannatyne, Rothesay in 1888 and remained working there until 1923. Another builder, John Thomson of Ardrossan, had served a seven-year apprenticeship at the same yard before setting himself up in business, and he built at least sixteen boats, most for the east Clyde fleet, which in all likelihood were of the nabbie-type, indistinguishable from the Lochfyne type in the registers.

The skiff *Fairy Queen*, CN128, in Campbeltown Loch, *c*.1930. She survives today on the West Coast of Ireland. (Photo courtesy of Mrs Margaret McKiernan.)

Campbeltown in the early years of the twentieth century..

Skiff *Three Brothers*. (Photo courtesy of Lachie Patterson.)

At least four of his boats went to Campbeltown. According to Angus Martin, Thomson's wife Isabella was part of the workforce. She worked from six in the morning to eight at night, after which she attended the needs of her family of twelve children. It is said that her skills matched those of any of the carpenters working in the yard.

The Fyfe family – relatives of the great yacht builder William Fife of Fairlie – had other members in the boatbuilding industry, other than John. Dan Fyfe worked under his own name in Tarbert after moving from Paisley, later moving to Stranraer. Robert Fyfe worked for a number of years at Ardrishaig, although he is believed to have worked in Tarbert for a short period as did his brother Thomas Fyfe.

The most prolific builders in Tarbert were Archibald Leitch, Archibald Dickie, Dugald and James Henderson and Alexander and Duncan McTavish while, in Ardrishaig, it was the Munro brothers, Archie and Donald, who built the most, the latter moving to Blairmore in 1908. It is said that they had at first commenced their boatbuilding together at Inveraray before moving to Ardrishaig in 1889, taking over the yard of James McLean, who was probably the most productive builder in Ardrishaig in those early years and who had also previously built many of the trawl skiffs.

The *Fame* at Dalintotser, Campbeltown. (Photo courtesy of Angus Martin.)

Robert Wylie of Campbeltown is perhaps the best known of all the builders on the west side of the Clyde, and maybe even further afield. He didn't commence building on his own account until 1893 when he launched the 27ft keel *Minnie Blair*, yet he was responsible for many innovations and technical developments mostly through his keenness as a yachtsman, crewing upon many of the larger racing yachts of the Clyde.

A few fishermen also mastered the art of building fishing boats. Matthew MacDougall of Port Righ, near Carradale, was one such man, building the *Isabella*, CN668, the *Mhairi*, CN130, the *Clan MacDougall*, CN9, the *Clan Matheson* and the *Maggie MacDougall*, CN65, between 1901 and 1906. Previous to that, he had built at least one large Campbeltown lugger, the *Mary & Agnes*, CN93, for himself at a time when several were being bought in from William Paynter's yard in St Ives, Cornwall, to sail to the Kinsale mackerel fishery off southern Ireland.

Clinker boatbuilding necessitated the forming of the shell of the boat over a set of temporary moulds, clenching each plank of timber to the previous one, beginning at the keel and bending the planks largely by eye to meet the stem and sternpost. Once the planking is completed, the internal frames are inserted to add strength to the hull, before fitting any half-deck, strengthening knees and internal work, mast, spars etc. Known as the 'shell-first' method, the clinker construction differs in some, especially Mediterranean, methods, in that the planks overlap, whereas other communities use ingenious ways of joining the planks end on. Clinker – sometimes called clench – boatbuilding is a method widely used today, especially in Scandinavia and northern Scotland. The first skiffs were built this way.

Waterfoot, Carradale.

The *Clan McNab*, TT138, built in 1922 and, at nearly 43ft long, the largest skiff built.
(Photo courtesy of Willie Crawford.)

Skiffs on Campbeltown New Quay.

A nabby from East … on the Clyde.
Postcard dated 1907.

A postcard of skiffs in Girvan harbour. (Photo courtesy of Mike Craine.)

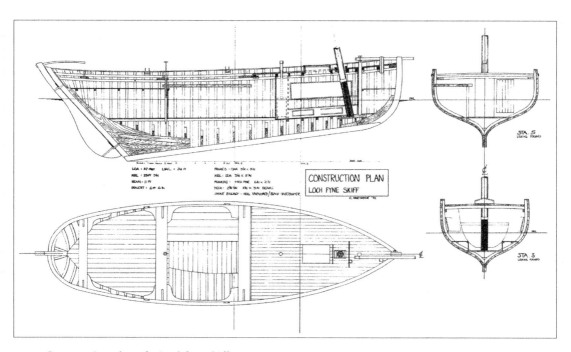

CONSTRUCTION PLAN
LOCH FYNE SKIFF

Construction plan of a Lochfyne skiff.

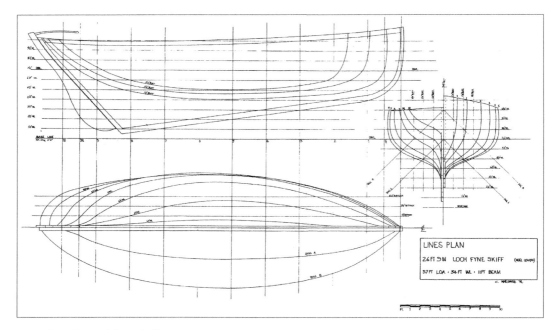

Line plan of a Lochfyne skiff.

Towards the end of the nineteenth century, carvel construction was introduced into the design of the skiffs. This method involves setting up the backbone of the hull – the keel, stem and sternpost – as before, but instead of using moulds, the frames are cut from oak and fixed onto the keel or keelson (a heavy piece of timber fixed on top of the keel). Each frame consists of separate pieces of oak, the floor being the piece lying across the keelson to which futtocks are fixed in the given shape of the vessel. Once the frames are completed and have been faired, planking commences with planks being fitted 'end to', and the gap between caulked to prevent water ingress. Once the planking is complete, work can begin on strengthening, the half-deck and internals as before. Advantages of this method are that larger and longer pieces of timber can be utilised, increasing the strength of the boat and its size.

Layout of a Skiff

A typical Lochfyne skiff was divided into three separate sections: the forecastle under the foredeck, the hold amidships and the stern sheets. Each section was divided by two stout crossbeams: the 'break of deck' where the foredeck ends, and the pump-beam between the hold and stern sheets, so-called because the bilge pump was attached to it. Below the pump-beam a bulkhead extended down to the planking of the hull. The stern sheets was, with sole timbers, the place to store the net and, at the after end, the stance for the helmsman at the tiller. A platform was built on the port side of the hold for the fishermen to stand upon whilst shooting and hauling the net. In the operation of the ring-net where two 'neighbour' boats work together, only one boat shoots the net when the presence of herring is detected.

Fleet of Lochfyne skiffs at Loch Ranza, Arran, preparing for sea, c.1910.

To detect the fish, fishermen used their knowledge of the so-called natural appearances, such as the presence of diving gannets, porpoises and basking sharks, oil on the sea or phosphorence. Once the net is shot with a dan-buoy attached at one end, the boat feeds it out around the shoal while the other boat picks up the dan-buoy. Both boats then proceed to tow – or trawl – the net for a short while before the ring is closed by the boats coming bow-to-stern alongside. At this point most of the crew of the second boat jump aboard the shooting boat to help with the hauling, completely enclosing the herring in the net by tightening the bottom ropes to form a sort of purse. Meanwhile the second boat tows the first boat to counteract any effect of wind and tide. Once the net is hauled in so that it sits between the two boats, the herring can be brailed aboard using a dip-net.

I hasten to add that one should not be deceived by how simple this technique sounds. Setting any net correctly needs experience, once the shoals are recognised, and hauling is a purely arduous task in which the hands are constantly wet and often in contact with jellyfish, referred to as 'scouders' by the fishermen and which left painful rashes. Added to this was the cold, the wind and the fact the skiffs were relatively small boats, all of which made ring-netting a dangerous occupation. These fishermen were true hunter-gatherers, using knowledge of seamanship passed down through generations. With the ring-net being in use for just over fifty years, during half of which it was banned, the fishermen were true pioneers. In fact, it can be said that ring-netting was a constantly evolving method due to improvements in the design and size of the net itself, the advent of motorisation which, in turn, led to innovations in the use of winches for hauling, the various ways developed to detect the herring (the Swedish feeling wire and, later, the echo-

Campbeltown herring fleet, c.1890.

Skiffs at Corrie on the east side of Arran.

The fleet at Campbeltown, *c.*1930.

Photograph – possibly of the *Janet* on the right – *c.*1919.

RING-NETTING ~ THE METHOD

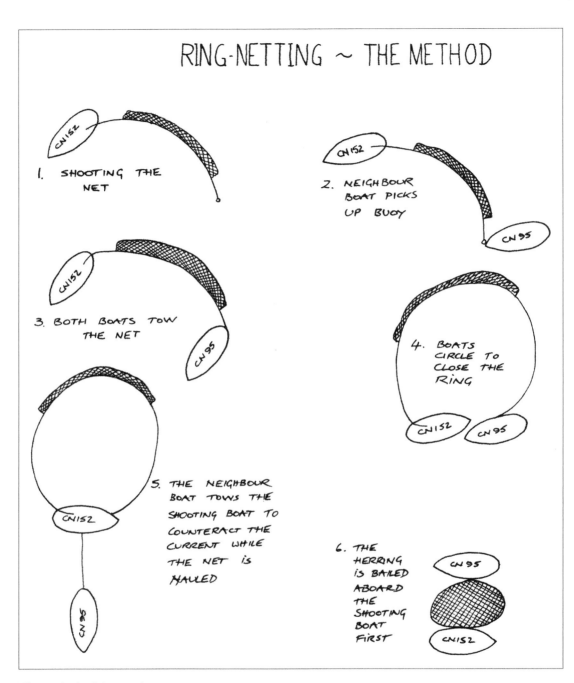

1. SHOOTING THE NET

2. NEIGHBOUR BOAT PICKS UP BUOY

3. BOTH BOATS TOW THE NET

4. BOATS CIRCLE TO CLOSE THE RING

5. THE NEIGHBOUR BOAT TOWS THE SHOOTING BOAT TO COUNTERACT THE CURRENT WHILE THE NET IS HAULED

6. THE HERRING IS BAILED ABOARD THE SHOOTING BOAT FIRST

The method of ring-netting.

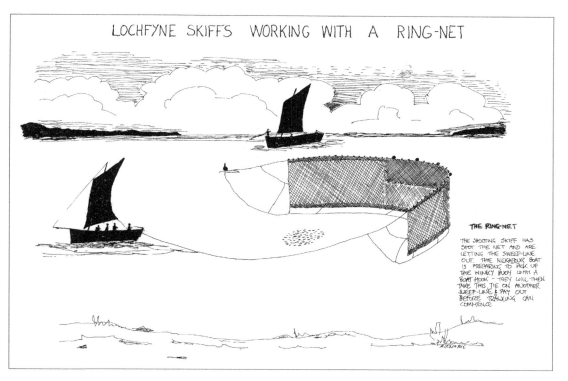

LOCHFYNE SKIFFS WORKING WITH A RING-NET

THE RING-NET

THE SHOOTING SKIFF HAS
SHOT THE NET AND ARE
LETTING THE SWEEP-LINE
OUT. THE NEIGHBOUR BOAT
IS PREPARING TO PICK UP
THE WINKY BUOY WITH A
BOAT HOOK – THEY WILL THEN
TAKE THIS, TIE ON ANOTHER
SWEEP-LINE & PAY OUT
BEFORE TRAWLING CAN
COMMENCE

Lochfyne skiffs working with a ring-net.

sounder and sonar) and changes in boats themselves, all of which continued right up to the 1970s when the last ring-net was set.

The forecastle, often referred to by the fishermen as the 'den', was able to accommodate four fishermen and a boy on four sleeping berths – two either side – while the boy slept on the floor. This was the normal crew of a skiff in Campbeltown, whereas Tarbert skiffs normally only had four crew in total. The berths consisted of two lockers, one either side, extending forward about 6ft from the bulkhead and acting as seats or as berths for two men. Below were lockers for storage. Above each locker was a hinged sleeping platform, usually made from a metal framework with a canvas base lashed to it. Usually kept in its upright position folded against the hull, it was dropped down at night and held in place by hooked metal rods.

At the forward end of the forecastle was another locker built into the forepeak. In the middle of the after bulkhead a stove was fitted – initially a fire hazard due to its proximity to the wooden bulkhead. As the size of the vessels increased from about 35ft upwards of 40ft, the forecastle increased correspondingly, up to about 14ft in length.

Improvements included using zinc or asbestos to protect the bulkhead to prevent burning of the timber. Around the beginning of the twentieth century improved 'Jack Tar' stoves were installed which had a guard rail around to prevent the kettle falling off. Coal was kept in a special locker in the hold. The stove allowed cooking although the menu was pretty mundane. Generally the diet consisted of herring and potatoes, when available, or other such delicacies as seabirds, all washed down with copious mugs of tea. Other basics such as bread and jam were

The Rescue, CN147, being presented to Dugold Muir (in stern) at Wylie's yard. *The Rescue* was built by public subscription after his old skiff was wrecked during a rescue of the *Davaar* in 1895. The notice reads: 'Presented to Dugald Muir by his fellow townsmen in recognition of his valuable services rendered Saving Seven Lives.'

brought aboard by the fishermen at the start of the week. Water was initially kept in a cask until metal water tanks were fitted under the stern sheets; they were later moved forward to the hold when engines were fitted in the stern sheets.

The forecastle was entered from the hold through a sliding door on the starboard side. The scuttle, through which the mast was positioned so that its foot rested on the mast step above the keel, acted as the entrance when the hold was full of herring, thus making entry by the sliding door impossible. It is said that the larger members of the crew, unable to squeeze down through the scuttle, had to remain on deck where they were passed warming cups of tea through the scuttle! Later skiffs had a hatch just aft of the mast scuttle.

Rig

The rig consisted of a standing lugsail, always set on the starboard side, attached to a high-peaked yard running on a traveller on the mast. The tack of the sail was attached to an iron horse fixed to the deck immediately in front of the mast. The clew was sheeted to bored holes in the top strake either side, just forward of the pump-beam. Unlike the dipping lugsail favoured by many other fishermen, such as those on the East Coast of Scotland or

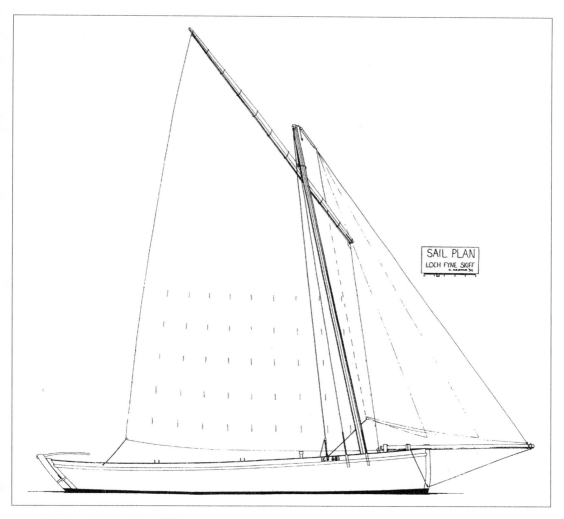

Sail plan of a Lochfyne skiff.

Cornwall, the standing lug did not need dipping around the mast and always remained set on the same side.

As mentioned previously, the Lochfyne skiffs were noted for their extreme backwards-raking of the mast. This was to allow the mast to be mounted further forward, thus creating as much space as possible amidships in the working area for setting and hauling the net and clearing the nets of fish. This rake, bringing the centre of effort aft, allowed a good windward performance and a handy response on the tiller, which was especially necessary when sailing close inshore, as ring-netting often demanded. When sailing with the wind, however, the opposite was true and improved performance was achieved by altering the angle of the mast to a more upright position. This was accomplished by moving the foot of the mast along a series of notches or tenons set into the mast step. The mast was supported by two shrouds on the starboard side and one on the port, with the lug-halyard acting as the second on that side. The lugsail had up to four reefing points.

RIGGING DETAILS

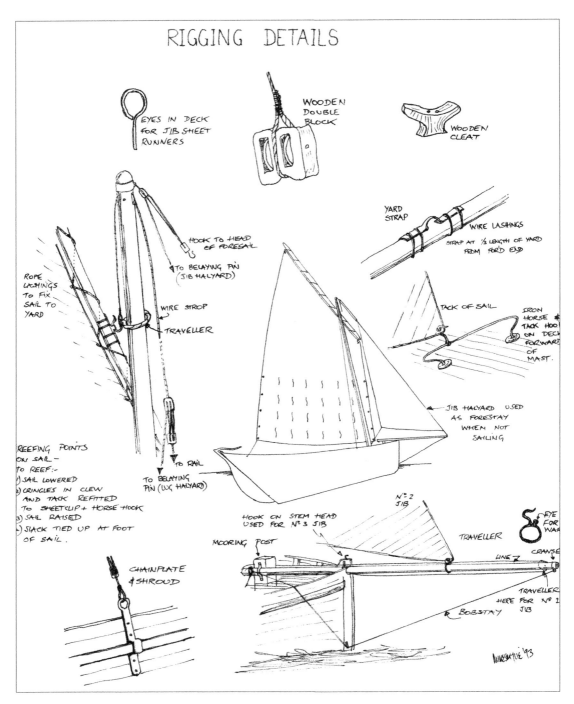

EYES IN DECK FOR JIB SHEET RUNNERS

WOODEN DOUBLE BLOCK

WOODEN CLEAT

HOOK TO HEAD OF FORESAIL

TO BELAYING PIN (JIB HALYARD)

ROPE LASHINGS TO FIX SAIL TO YARD

WIRE STROP

TRAVELLER

YARD STRAP

WIRE LASHINGS

STRAP AT ⅓ LENGTH OF YARD FROM FORD END

TACK OF SAIL

IRON HORSE & TACK HOOK ON DECK FORWARD OF MAST.

JIB HALYARD USED AS FORESTAY WHEN NOT SAILING

REEFING POINTS ON SAIL —
TO REEF:-
1) SAIL LOWERED
2) CRINGLES IN CLEW AND TACK REFITTED TO SHEETCLIP + HORSE HOOK
3) SAIL RAISED
4) SLACK TIED UP AT FOOT OF SAIL.

TO RAIL

TO BELAYING PIN (LUG HALYARD)

CHAINPLATE & SHROUD

HOOK ON STEM HEAD USED FOR Nº 3 JIB

MOORING POST

Nº 2 JIB

TRAVELLER

EYE FOR WAR

LINE

CRANSE

TRAVELLER HERE FOR Nº 1 JIB

BOBSTAY

Niko Battie '93

Rigging details.

The jib was set by line on a traveller running along the bowsprit and leading through a block at the end of the bowsprit. The bowsprit was always brought inboard when fishing to prevent entanglement when the neighbouring skiff came alongside, and was only shipped outboard when making passage or returning home in light winds.

Sails were tanned when new and then up to three times a year to prevent rot. This was done by setting the sail out on a flat surface and brushing a cutch solution, with added fat. Once one side was completed, the sail would be folded into itself, progressively exposing the whole of the underside which was also coated until both sides of the entire sail were tanned. This was left for a few days to soak in before being attached to the yard and hauled up the mast to dry. The cutch solution was the same as that used to bark the nets to preserve them from salt-water rot. Before the import of cutch – made from the acacia tree of South East Asia – oak bark was the preferred tannin. Fat was added to the tanning solution to help the tannin to hold into the sail. Other ingredients sometimes added were horse manure, dog muck and rancid butter.

Upkeep and Decline

Once a year, usually in the early autumn, the fishermen would race against each other, testing the skills of both boat and crew. For the premier race racing sails, used solely for the purpose, would be rigged. The boats were scrubbed clean and a coat of black lead brushed on, sometimes over two coats of varnish or oil, to help them glide through the water.

Other than this treatment, the skiffs were well cared for at all times for they were a major investment for most fishermen. Each spring or early summer the skiffs would be beached for up to three weeks and their hulls scrubbed of any marine growth and recoated with coal tar or varnish. Internally everything was scrubbed and varnished while, every two or three years, all the ballast – the skiffs used up to 2 tons of sandbags or stones as ballast – was removed and the inside of the hull coated in boiled linseed oil. Sweeps, used for rowing the vessels, were also thus treated. The practice of keeping their hulls varnished, for which the Loch Fyne and Campbeltown vessels were renowned, continued well into the twentieth century.

A word about rowing: at times when the wind was non-existent, it was normal practice to row using the long sweeps that were up to 25ft in length. Two men rowed with one oar each, the boy sometimes helping with a shorter oar. It was not abnormal to have to row home under such conditions which could take several hours.

'Going out to the fields of herring.'

Old–timers!

Half-decked smacks on the beach by Loch Ranza Castle, Arran.

More half-decked smacks in this postcard of Blackwaterfoot, Arran.

Typical Campbeltown-registered skiff under mainsail.

Angus Martin McBride, 1932. (Photo courtesy of Mrs Margaret McBride Harvison, of Pirnmill.)

Mary, 247CN, a clinker-built skiff, built by Lachie Lang in 1884.

Good Hope, skippered by Hugh MacLean, in regatta rig. Built in 1906 by D. Munro of Inveraray, she was sold to Stranraer in 1934. (Photo courtesy of Angus Martin.)

Gilchrist skiff *Mary McLemman*, built in Ardrossan in 1901, under sail.

The skiff *Three Brothers*, CN170. (Photo courtesy of Lachie Patterson.)

In the words of Angus Martin, 'the final development of the trawl-fishing began in 1907 with the installation of a 7–9hp Kelvin petrol/paraffin engine in the *Brothers*, a Campbeltown skiff almost 35 feet in length and built in 1900 by John Thomson of Ardrossan'. Not only was this the first motor-powered fishing boat in the Campbeltown fleet, but also on the whole of the Scottish West Coast, and thus a move of great significance: whilst being the beginning of the final development of ring-netting, the introduction of the motor-powered fishing boat also signalled the demise of the skiffs. The development of the Kelvin engine will now be considered, before the decline and ultimate disappearance of the Lochfyne skiff in the fishing fleets is explored.

five

The Fisherman's Friend –
The Kelvin Engine

This chapter is dedicated to the memory of George Bergius who has sadly died since it was first written in 1998. George proof-read this chapter before it appeared as an article in Classic Boat *magazine.*

The 'fisherman's friend' isn't just a particular brand of well-known lozenge, it's a development that had far-reaching effects upon fishermen the world over and which came in the form of the internal combustion engine. On the West Coast of Scotland the fisherman's friend was the Kelvin engine.

Anyone with any experience of working boats on the West Coast carries a healthy respect for the Kelvin name, and this was especially true of the fishermen. This is hardly surprising since the company that introduced the Kelvin grew and flourished alongside changes in the fishing industry from the earliest days of the twentieth century. This association continued right into the second half of the century when, in 1965, out of sixty-seven fishing boats built that year, twenty-six had Kelvins fitted. Out of the total 11,186hp supplied, 4,656hp was Kelvin power.

The story of Kelvin engines began unpretentiously in a first-floor workshop in the middle of Glasgow. Number 169 Finnieston Street had previously been home to J. & G. Thomson, which later became part of John Brown Shipbuilders (famous for their transatlantic liners) and the Albion Motor Company, makers of the Albion lorry. Kelvins then, far from originating in the damp, windy waters of the West Coast, first breathed life under the bonnet of motor cars.

In 1904 Walter Bergius, then only twenty-three years old, founded the Bergius Car and Engine Company. Although the internal combustion engines were put into motor vehicles in the 1880s, the first cars as we know them didn't arrive until the very beginning of the twentieth century, the 1902 Wolseley being one of the first. There was a rush in the ensuing years to produce cars and the young Bergius was keen to profit from the stampede.

Walter Bergius was directly related to the great whisky-distilling family, the Teachers, from whom he presumably got funding to begin his enterprise. His elder brother, Willie, worked for the company and suggested to David Willocks (a dissatisfied employee who wanted to become an engineer) that he talk to Walter.

To Walter, it was a boom or bust idea to build engines, but nevertheless the young David joined and remained with the company until well after Walter's death, succeeding him as chairman and managing director. David quickly became the commercial head of the new company after his departure from the whisky empire, 'keeping the books when his hands were clean' in his own words. George Rutherford became the pattern-maker, Willie Hunt the machinist and Jack Muir

The cover of an early Kelvin catalogue.

Walter Bergius.

the assistant, although he only stayed a few months. The weekly wage bill was £4 1s 6d and they worked a fifty-four-hour week. The general rate was 8d an hour or 36s a week.

The building was completely unsuited to car manufacturing. The entrance to the first-floor premises was by outdoor wooden stairs, so that all the incoming goods had to be hoisted up. The Finnieston Engineering Company, which occupied the ground floor below and regularly left their wheelbarrow under the hoist so that it was flattened by the descending contraption, made all the Kelvin fuel tanks for well over fifty years. There was no heating and only gas lighting. The principal machinery was a centre-lathe that had cost £66, driven by a 9hp gas engine of uncertain age. The annual rent was £75 and the total plant was insured for £500.

They called their engine Kelvin, after the river that runs through part of the city. Lord Kelvin, the renowned scientist and inventor, had taken the name and Glasgow still has a Kelvingrove Park.

The first car had a wooden body with a rear entrance and wooden wheels with solid rubber tyres. It was ready by Christmas 1904, having taken seven months to build. Each component from the engine and transmission, to the axles, wheels, radiator and bodywork, were made on the premises. Everything had to be cast, turned or fabricated.

However, disaster struck on the first test. Only yards into its first journey, the piston punched part of the ignition through the cylinder head. This was then redesigned and rebuilt in three weeks to the 3in pattern that was to become a permanent sizing for subsequent engines. Second time round it worked, and worked well, so that three more cars were built which were identical

The first Kelvin car, of 1906.

The first Kelvin launch catalogue.

A 25ft Kelvin launch, carvel-built in mahogany by Leith & McCallum of Renfrew in 1907.

The first launch – the *Kelvin*.

but for having pneumatic tyres. The previous rubber tyres were thin, and the axle size the same as the gauge of the Glasgow tramlines. Accordingly, the first car tended to get jammed in the rails, and couldn't be steered away.

The first car was sold to Mr McKean, who drove it to London himself without mishap, obviously avoiding the trams! Walter Bergius' father bought the second, and a Mr Hunter the third. At the time the cost of one of these cars was £350, and an engine could be bought for £70. During the Scottish Reliability Trials in 1906, the car – with its 16hp at 950rpm engine – achieved a fuel consumption of 22.56mpg over the 1,000 miles.

Sales, however, weren't outstanding due to competition from such famous names as Rover, Humber, Daimler and Argyll, all of which were growing rapidly at that time. Later that year, Willie Bergius suggested the installation of one of the engines into a 23ft rowing gig, and they soon found that they had built a winner. Naturally they called this boat *Kelvin*. The two brothers had previously built a boat when Walter was seventeen years old – in their bedroom at home. This boat, *Dodo*, remains in the Scottish Maritime Museum at Irvine.

Walter realised the massive impact this success might have on the West Coast fishing fleets and so production of the car was abandoned in favour of marine engines and launches. An advert was placed in *Motor Boat* in 1906, and the company built *Kelvin II*, which won even more races than her predecessor. The launches were mahogany built, and to begin with there was only one choice: 23ft long by 5ft beam.

Also in 1906 J. & G. Forbes, fishing boatbuilders of Sandhaven on the East Coast, bought a four-cylinder engine. Two more were sold to Oban and the first exported to New Zealand in 1907. That same year the first fishing boat on the West Coast had an engine fitted at a cost of £70 complete. After three years of trading, the firm had sold fifteen cars, nine launches and sixty-seven marine engines – twenty-two of which were exported to Australia, New Zealand, Bombay, Russia, Bangkok, Norway, Uruguay, Trinidad, Cochin, Hong Kong and Fiji. In the words of David Willocks, 'not bad, starting from scratch'.

Walter Bergius was evidently an extraordinary man, a born engineer, devoted to his ideas, extremely hard working, and a good employer. He was methodical and intolerant of things that were non-standard. In the dawning days of British Standards, when hardly anything from a nut and bolt to the section of electrical cable was standardised, he created his own standard. Everything he ordered was of a particular size, to a Bergius company drawing number, and remained so. Several companies he dealt with were forced to do the same.

He was also an individualist who believed in his own knowledge and experience but at the same time he realised his own limitation; he was in the driving seat, yet was always covered in oil. He drove the business forward, enabling it to adapt, grow and benefit during a time when engineering was developing at high speed in Britain. The results are visible today in thousands of boats of all types all over the world.

The Kelvin Launch

In 1906, in the hope of capitalising on the success of the Kelvin launches, Walter instructed his pattern-maker to build a launch he had designed. A competent naval architect as well as an engineer, the result was a light, mahogany-built, fine craft. This was immediately shipped to Australia in the December of that year.

The advert in *Motor Boat* quotes this launch as costing £215 with a four-cylinder engine and £185 for the two-cylinder version. With the engines alone costing £100 and £70 respectively, the launches themselves were therefore costing £115 apiece. The engines had mahogany covers, and copper funnels were fitted as standard. Their maximum speed was stated as being 11 knots.

In 1908 the company name changed to the Bergius Launch and Engine Company. By this time the range had increased to include a 25ft standard pleasure launch, a 22ft and 26ft utility launch and a 16ft yacht pinnace. These were all supplied with Kelvin engines and reverse gear, and at the suggestion of Willie Bergius, the company also developed and patented a Kelvin folding propeller. The same stern gear was fitted to the fishing fleets, which by now were adopting motorised units from the company. Turnover in 1908 rose to about £10,000 and in the following year jumped to £21,000.

George Rutherford, the pattern-maker, emigrated to New South Wales, Australia, about this time and became the company agent out there. A network of agents was set up all around the world, and to commemorate this, in 1914 the company produced a photograph with all thirty-eight of its staff and agents around the world. There were some thirty agents in Britain, with others in exotic spots such as Siberia, Natal in South Africa, Tasmania, Burma, Argentina, China, Trieste, Portugal and Denmark.

In 1910 the company moved to the premises with which it was to become identified: 254 Dobbies Loan. Every West Coast fisherman would have been there at one time or another, and any mention of Dobbies Loan still evokes nostalgia in many fishermen on this coast and further afield today. The new site covered one acre and provided more space, allowing greater flexibility to extend the range further.

The launch catalogue No. 4, dated 1913, gives a good idea of the available range of launches in pine or teak, and sometimes even steel, all with a choice of engines. These launches were built by various boatbuilders around the UK, and later in Norway. The hulls were delivered to

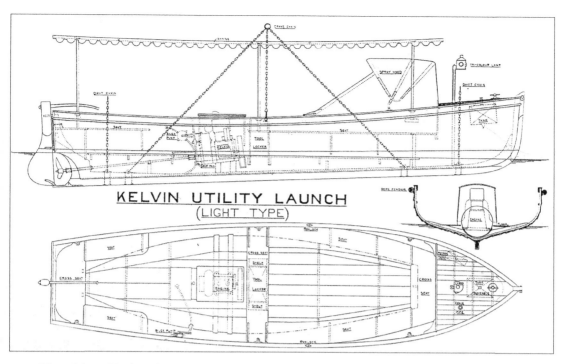

KELVIN UTILITY LAUNCH
(LIGHT TYPE)

Plan of the utility launch.

the Bergius boatshed at Port Dundas (on the Monklands branch of the Forth & Clyde Canal), which was in operation by about 1913. They were then fitted out with engines and finished before being sold on.

The wooden launches were either clinker- or carvel-built, with oak centrelines, keel, ribs and rubbing strake in elm and finished in either teak or mahogany. Copper sheathing below the waterline was an option costing between £12 and £30, depending on the size of vessel, and one taken up by many of the overseas customers. They could also be supplied complete with awnings (approx. £12), a brass steering-wheel (£6) and even a 'closet' (£10). The catalogue advertises the launches as being suitable for 'missionaries, planters, fishermen, pilots and all general purposes'.

The 'substantially built, luxurious' cabin launches were the top of the range, having a lavatory, cooker, saloon and two berths, with the largest having a third berth over the engine for an engineer. Thomas Fleming Day, who twice crossed the Atlantic in a small boat, the second time in the sharp-sterned *Detroit*, wrote, 'I do assert that a properly designed square stern for sea work is far better than any sharp stern'. His opinion vindicated the adoption of the transom in these launches and helped increase their general acceptance.

After the end of the First World War, encouraged by the sales of the poppet-valve engines, the company added to the range of launches. Amongst these were the service launches, despatch launches, beach boats, naval pinnaces, ferry launches, fishing launches, water boats, passenger launches and, for use in tropical climates, the Kelvin houseboat. Prices for the latter ranged from £742 for the 42ft pine-built, 26hp petrol-engined version to £934 for the 42ft teak-built, 30hp paraffin-engined, while £35 would copper sheath the hull of either. The 22ft light utility

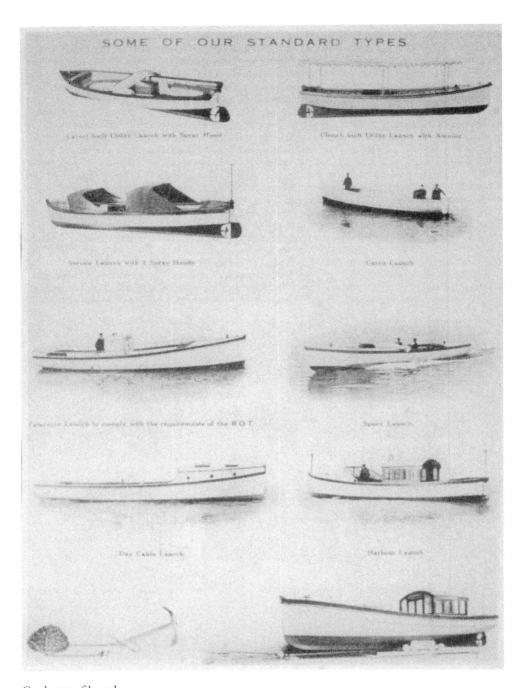

Catalogue of launches.

40′ x 9′ UTILITY LAUNCH

22′ x 6′ UTILITY LAUNCH

26′ x 6′ SERVICE LAUNCH

23′ x 7′ TOWING LAUNCH

28′ x 6′ 6″ DAY CABIN LAUNCH

40′ x 10′ GENERAL SERVICE LAUNCH

30′ x 8′ SURF LAUNCH

32′ x 8′ HARBOUR LAUNCH

JAMES N. MILLER & SONS LTD.
ST. MONANCE - FIFE

Kelvin launches from Millers of St Monans.

A Kelvin launch.

launch, the bottom of the range, cost only £122, complete with a 3hp petrol engine. This was considerably cheaper then the 1906 boat, since the company had been able to cut costs by securing favourable terms from the builders. This was all part of Walter Bergius' drive for standardisation, and some thirty were always available from stock. By 1939, however, the range was slightly reduced as the company concentrated on engine building. Prices had risen with a 26ft pine service launch up from £179 in 1919 to £265, a rise of about 50 per cent.

A 'commodious family cruiser' was added, with a hull similar to the fast developing MFV hull. This was 48ft long by 15ft beam, and was fitted out with eight bunks, galley and toilet. The rigged boat, complete with a 44hp K2 diesel, cost under £2,000.

By 1940 the company had sold about 1,500 launches. The majority went for export – the largest customers were the Crown Agents for the colonies and Gray, Dawes & Co. West Africa. Yet Walter Bergius decided enough was enough and gave all the plans for the drawings to Willie Miller of James N. Miller & Sons of St Monans, who had previously been employed as an office boy at Dobbies Loan. Millers marketed the range under the name Miller-Kelvin Launches alongside their own renowned Fifer Fishing Craft, and continued supplying harbour launches, towing launches, general service launches, cabin launches, customs and ambulance launches, passenger and cargo launches and utility launches. Kelvin engines, stern gear and steering all remained standard. The range survived in the 1960s, yet, for Kelvins, abandoning the launches enabled them to develop and expand the range of their successful engines.

The Kelvin Engine

The early Kelvin motors were extremely simple and easy to use. They had no clutch or reverse gear, and were perfectly suited to the fishermen who didn't have the time to constantly tinker with their engines while they were fishing. As previously mentioned, the first unit to go into the West Coast fleet in 1907 was in the Lochfyne skiff *Brothers*, CN97, owned by one of the most innovative of British fishermen, Robert Robertson. We shall see in the next chapter how he later went on to alter the shape of fishing craft by building the first canoe-sterned ringers, *Falcon* and *Frigate Bird*, that arguably were the forerunners to the Scottish MFVs which dominated fishing for most of the twentieth century. His 7-9hp engine had cost £50, with another £20 being charged for the unit to be installed.

The following year saw many skiffs having motors fitted. The units were secured into the stern sheets on the starboard side because the net was always shot to port; the hull was strengthened with blocks of timber, and the compartment covered over. By the end of the year some ten West Coast fishing vessels had motor units, six being Campbeltown boats. Out of these latter, four had Kelvins, one had a 7hp Thornycroft paraffin engine installed at a cost of £95 and the other an 11hp Fairbank for £86. The Kelvin units produced a speed of between 4 and 5 knots, while the Fairbanks gave 6 knots. This engine had the added advantage of a reverse gear, although the fishermen tended not to be particularly bothered with this.

Kelvins were fitted to an Inveraray and a Ballantrae skiff, while a Rothesay skiff was built with a single-cylinder Gardner, this unit costing £110 while the boat itself only cost £75. The Kyleakin vessel, *General de Wet*, had a two-cylinder Gardner at a cost of £375. Although

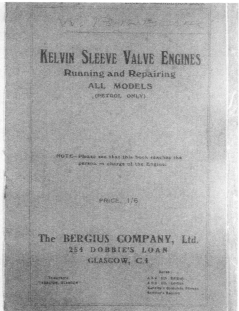

Covers of Kelvin engine handbooks.

Cover of Kelvin Ricardo catalogue.

this latter engine was deemed expensive, especially compared to the Kelvins, the boat reached a speed of 8 knots and was often the first boat back to catch the fish train at Kyle of Lochalsh.

But Kelvins were the most popular. They were relatively efficient and reliable, and still the cheapest. Most of the conversions were done by James Litster at Hunter's Quay Pier, Dunoon. Litster's asked for £35 at the time of installation and the remaining £35 over the next year. This allowed the fishermen to make payments as catches improved.

Walter Bergius also had a strong belief in the need to back up sales with a forceful spares service. The company advertised that an order for spares received by the first post would be dispatched the same day. Fifty per cent of orders received in the second post were also sent out the same day. This service was of the utmost importance to the fishermen, who would otherwise have to sit in port awaiting spare parts.

By the time the company had moved to 254 Dobbies Loan in 1910, some eighty-one fishing vessels had had motors fitted. A year later no pair of sailing fishing boats remained in Campbeltown, and in 1912 there were seventy-two motor boats in the fleet. That year *Perseverance*, CN152, emerged from Robert Wylie's yard, with her 13.15 poppet-valve engine. By the next year there were seven models of the poppet-valve engine from 3–60hp. Paraffin, the same year, cost up to 8*d* per gallon, a 100 per cent increase on the price of a few years earlier. In 1919, a 26hp unit cost £351.

So far we've only considered the fishing boats from the West Coast of Scotland, however the company was making inroads all around the country. By the time war broke out in 1914, there were about 1,000 fishing boats with Kelvin engines. Agents were installed around the Scottish

Auxiliary Power
For Sailing Yachts and Fishing Boats.

The Bergius Side Propeller System.

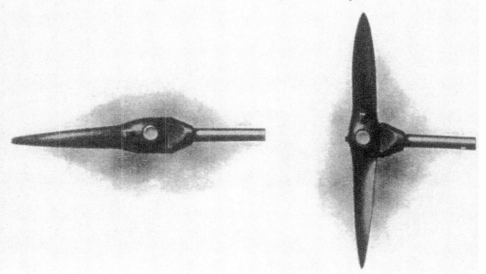

Auxiliary power catalogue.

East Coast – at Wick, Gourdon, St Monans and in the Shetlands – while Cornwall adopted the engines with agents at Mousehole, Mevagissey, Polperro, Gorran Haven, St Mawes, Looe and Plymouth – as well as the renowned J.T. Cowls of Porthleven, whom I visited a few years ago to view his collection of old Kelvins. The boatbuilders Watterson & Neakle of Peel, Isle of Man, were recognised agents and fitted many Kelvins into the Manx fleet. Grimsby, Hastings and Folkestone had agents, and, of course, there were those world-wide agents already mentioned.

The company wasn't about to sit on its laurels, however, and Walter Bergius was keen to develop another range of quieter engines. The poppet-valve engine was undoubtedly successful – from its inception to the final engine built in 1960 there were 16,500 of them made – but to compete with these the sleeve-valve range was launched in 1920. In order to cope with increased production, the company bought premises at Stafford Street which became the machine shop and foundry.

The sleeve-valve units were much quieter and were fitted into working boats and pleasure yachts in all corners. Many boats had their poppet-valve engines removed in favour of the new units. *Perseverance* had a two-cylinder C2, 30hp sleeve-valve engine fitted about 1928 and soon gained fame amongst the fleets.

That the sleeve-valve engines were deemed an improvement on the older engines is attested to by the large number of conversions over a short period. The smallest unit, the A2 7½hp cost £80, while the biggest, the C4 60hp, was £450. Its quietness is reflected in a Girvan story of a fisherman who arrived on his boat on a Monday morning to find his engine running. So quietly was it ticking over that nobody had noticed on the Friday as they left for home!

The testing shop at Dobbies Loan.

Photographs of all the Kelvin
agents in a 1914 poster.

In 1927 the Kelvin–Ricardo engine was launched. Harry Ricardo was a consulting engineer who had been employed by the government during the war to design engines for tanks and was eventually knighted for his work. He designed his own combustion chambers in the cylinder head, which were incorporated into the Kelvin engine. Again, six models of the Kelvin–Ricardo were available, a two- and four-cylinder version of E, F and G, which were 3in, 4in and 5in bore respectively.

The first G4 60hp was fitted into the Newfoundland schooner *Neptune II* after it had been blown across the Atlantic in a storm in 1930. After forty-eight days adrift it had fetched up off Ardnamurchan Point and was subsequently towed to Oban. The master, Job Barbour, contacted Walter Bergius, and the engine was fitted accordingly. The boat re-crossed homewards under full power in twenty days without mishap. Four years later it voyaged to Oporto with a cargo of fish, and back again, a journey of 4,850 miles, and the engine didn't falter once. This story is told in the book *48 Days Adrift* by Cap. Job Barbour.

Although we've only considered working boats so far, it is worth mentioning that hundreds of sailing yachts and motor boats also had Kelvins fitted. By the time of the First World War, there were 250 boats with the units. An advert in the 1930s Lloyd's Register of Yachts makes interesting reading. It states that in the previous year's register, the number of Kelvins detailed exceeds the combined total of any other three makes by over one hundred engines.

The first sailing yacht to have a Kelvin engine fitted was the 28ft bermudan sloop *Dodo II* in 1906. Designed by Willie Bergius, she had been built by James Lister at Kirn in 1903. The original 6hp engine, with low tension ignition, was only replaced in 1936 by a model E2 7hp Kelvin–Ricardo. This first engine is presently in the safe-keeping of the Glasgow Museum of Transport at the Kelvin Hall.

Mediterranean fishing boat with Kelvin engine.

A Maltese fishing boat fitted with a Kelvin 30hp sleeve-valve.

One of the better-known yachts fitted with Kelvin engines was the twin-screwed 47ft *Silver Strand*, which featured in the *Para Handy* television series as the puffer owner's yacht. Built in 1926 by McLaren Bros of Dumbarton as *Maudorces 2*, she had a four-cylinder 30hp Kelvin sleeve-valve paraffin engine amidships and a 15hp sleeve-valve as a side engine.

Still the company didn't rest. In 1932 it advertised in the *Motor Boat* magazine that it had, over the previous twenty-five years, taken part in the pioneering work of converting the British fishing fleet to petrol/paraffin engines, and now was introducing the diesel engine. Consequently the J and K range of engines were launched, and became the real breadwinners for the company. They found immediate favour amongst the fishermen. The *Perseverance* was taken to the boatshed at Port Dundas and thence to the Maryhill dry-dock for out-of-the-water work to form a central aperture and installation of the J4 44hp, the same engine the boat had when I sold her. The new engine was no. 20445, and it is solely because of Walter Bergius' extremely careful and detailed cataloguing of all engines that I now have the full details of the engine, its installation and testing. Indeed, until recently when the company destroyed records up to engine no. 20800, any engine could be traced. The original folios I've seen – Book One being from engine No. 334, December 1909 to No. 692, 1 January 1911 – give the engine type, shop order number and date sent out, as well as remarks about the unit.

During the Second World War, the K4s were fitted into the 61ft 6in Admiralty MFVs and the F4s into the harbour launches. They were fitted exclusively into the small craft that carried out commando raids on the Lofoten Islands, the company personnel servicing them prior to the raid. Again the company emerged from the war with distinction.

One design feature of these engines was their ability to be started using petrol. A brass carburettor sits atop the engine and a rail leads the fuel to a separate chamber where a small lever makes the changeover. The injectors are turned off and the carburettor filled with a special measure of petrol. A magneto produces a spark as soon as the engine is turned over, and it runs on petrol until the diesel is switched on.

Many a damp magneto refused to produce a spark, so that most fishermen tended to keep theirs at home in the oven until required, but the system ensured that many an engine did start by hand, when other makes refused. Again this was pioneering engineering by Walter Bergius himself. The simplicity of the units was their strength, so that most work could be done by almost anyone.

Many of these diesel engines were adapted as stationary units, the most popular application being in the Northern Lights lighthouses, where both K2 and K3 engines drove compressor units for the fog horns. These engines were kept in pristine condition, many only being run for twenty minutes a week, unless there was fog. Yet when they were removed they were merely, in many cases, tipped over the cliff into the sea.

By this time, all sorts of boats had Kelvins fitted – from barges and fishing boats in this country to Mediterranean Gozo boats, Fijian tuna boats, Kenyan pilot boats, Saudi Arabian trading dhows, Japanese-built Indian ore barges, Egyptian hotel ships, and fishing boats from Hong Kong, Africa and South America.

Walter Bergius died in 1949 at the age of sixty-eight. Four years later the family sold out his 96 per cent share holding to the Brush-ABE Group, part of which became Associated British Engineering that included the Bergius company. The freshwater range that he was developing continued, and a new range was launched under the auspices of W.N. Miller, who was previously the chief development officer at Petter Diesels, and this mono block version became the P range.

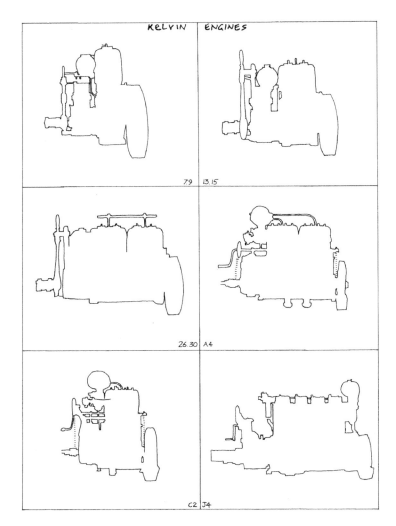

KELVIN ENGINES

7.9　13.15

26.30　A4

C2　J4

Kelvin engines.

The P and R ranges survived most of the various changes of ownership (and names) of the company, culminating in its acquisition in 1994 by Lincoln Diesels, who restored the Kelvin name. The model P range had finally been discontinued in 1980, but the R range continued until as recently as 1991. The world-renowned Dobbies Loan factory was sold in 1993.

The company moved to modern premises at Tannochside Park, Uddington, just outside Glasgow, which were opened by the then trade minister Lord George Younger. I had a tour a couple of years ago and found them with plenty of room and scope to expand as they continue to manufacture the T range. Kelvin's predominant markets over the last thirty years have been the UK, Greece, Norway, West and East Africa, the Middle East, the Far East, Australia and the Pacific Islands.

That, then, is the story of the Bergius company. During the time I was researching its history of the last ninety years or so, I met up with George Bergius on several occasions, without whose help I couldn't have written this. He joined the company in 1939 as an apprentice at the age

Scottish ferry with modern Kelvin engine fitted.

of seventeen. Being Walter Bergius' son, this apprentice lasted twice as long as anyone else's. He then spent six months pattern-making, six months in the boatshed fitting the units, and then another six months – to his dismay to begin with – in the stores. Yet here he learnt more than perhaps anywhere else: the names of parts, their use, where they were made and their values, so that today he thinks that the stores were the mainstay of the business.

We talked about his father's belief in maintaining a strong spares service, and he told me about the time when the Kelvin agent in Reykjavik telegraphed for spares for a British boat fishing in Icelandic waters. His father told him to take the parts to Glasgow airport himself and put them on the flight to Iceland. When the boat limped back into Reykjavik, the spares were waiting on the quay.

He showed me photos of his father's yacht *Vaillima II*, designed by him and built by Silvers in 1926. At nearly 80ft overall, she was described by Uffa Fox in his book *Sail and Power* as being one of the most successful vessels ever designed. He regarded her as a proper 50/50, one that sails as well as it motors. She had sufficient rig to power her along at 10 knots and win races, yet her 66hp K3 equally pushed her through the water at speed.

George remembers the two weeks they spent on the boat each summer, cruising the Western Isles, arguably the best cruising ground in Europe, if you ignore the weather! When visitors, fishermen or friends came aboard to admire the boat, especially the engine, he would ask them if they'd like to hear it running. 'Right,' he'd say, 'I'll get the boy.' Down George would run, switch over the decompression levers to petrol, swing the engine and away it would go: the job of the 'boy' in his early teens.

Skiff *Three Brothers* soon after having engine installed, *c.*1910.

George and his wife had spent a week aboard *Vaillima II* cruising the Aegean, only the year I met them. Although she remains much as she was, *Vaillima II* now has a Kelvin R6, 150hp main engine.

George has an amazing collection of catalogues and other company literature. They brought back memories of me sitting crouched in *Perseverance*'s engine room, the smell of the J4 engine, with the manual in one hand as I battled to start her using the petrol, when, of course, the magneto was wet!

But the most interesting feature is apparent from even the early catalogues. Each launch, each engine and each extra was given a five-letter code word. The code for the 60hp heavy-type four-cylinder model, with shaft supplied for a 2ft-thick sternpost, is 'BABIT' and for the 6ft version, 'BABON'. Turning to the engine price sheet F, issued on 11 December 1915, I find the above words and alongside a current price, £430 and £438.

Code words were given to spares, and even to prearranged enquiries for engine prices and shipment dates. A telegram might read, 'Bergius, Glasgow – Gehanbagan – Jones, New York', meaning 'what is your price packed and delivered here, and how soon can you have ready for shipment, 26hp equipment as per page 8 – Jones, New York'.

Skiff *Ellen*, neighbour boat to *Perseverance*, returning from Hunter's Quay after the installation of a Kelvin engine in 1908.

The reply might be, 'Jones, New York – Gisam 225, Gotozgobia – Bergius', meaning 'price packed and delivered New York is £225. Ready for shipment now, if you remit 10 per cent by telegraph we will ship by first steamer and collect balance against bill of loading at port of destination – Bergius'.

There are still many engines from the Bergius company running toady. Only recently I was aboard the newly restored fifie *Isabella Fortuna* and saw her K3. The Kelvin Register, as well as being a source of research material, supplies rebuilt engines and produces a bimonthly magazine focusing on all aspects of Kelvin engines. New units continue to be manufactured, with recent developments concerning the Kelvin launches being the icing to the cake, so to speak.

Although I found one or two surviving launches during my travels, including one not many miles from home, and another rotting in a field to the north-east of Anglesey, there don't appear to be that many in working order. It's encouraging, then, from a maritime historical point of view, that lottery funding was awarded to the Edinburgh Canal Society for the rebuilding of a 22ft utility launch that they discovered on the beach at Fisherrow several years ago. This was fitted with an original Kelvin-Ricardo E2 engine and launched in 2002; it still sails today on the Union Canal. I've also heard of a completely new clinker utility launch being built at Johnshaven, on the East Coast of Scotland, on spec. Furthermore, exhibitions of Kelvin engines such as Billy Stevenson's at Newlyn, make it obvious that Kelvins continue to interest people from all walks of life. In 2004 the Bergius company celebrated its centenary with another range of engines that have taken it into the twenty-first century. Nothing else could be a more fitting epitaph to Walter Bergius' pioneering work that led to one of the most important innovations to benefit our fishing fleets – the fisherman's friend. There were, of course, other engines that have become synonymous with fishing such as Gardner and Thornycroft engines, but the Kelvin has always remained favourite amongst the ring-netters of Loch Fyne; thus their inclusion here is warranted for that very reason.

[Kelvin Diesels is today owned by Associated British Engineering plc.]

six

The Advent of Motorisation and the Decline of the Skiffs

The changing face of motorisation was incorporated into the fishing fleets on the Clyde, but with, no doubt, a lack of enthusiasm on the part of some of the fishermen. However, much in the same way that the doubters regarded the change from drift- to ring-net with suspicion or the addition of decks to their vessels, in a relatively short time these suspicions gave way and almost all the Lochfyne skiffs were converted to motor power, whilst all new skiffs were installed with motor power at the outset. Because of the configuration of the sternpost and the impracticality of boring it out, the engines were aligned so that the propeller shaft emerged out on the starboard side of the vessel and this was, ultimately, one reason why motorised skiffs did not have a long lifespan in comparison with other Scottish types, such as the East Coast fifie. The vertical sternpost of the fifie adapted easily to having a shaft through it and a large propeller aperture built into the sternpost and rudder.

Robert Wylie's first motor-boat conversion was the *Lady Carrick Buchanan*, CN38, of Carradale, fitted with a Thornycroft 7½hp unit in 1908, four years after he had built her. The same year saw Duncan 'Captain' Wilkinson's *Ellen*, CN97, the *Perseverance*'s neighbour boat, having a Kelvin fitted at Hunter's Quay, not long after she'd been built. After Wylie launched the *Perseverance* in 1912, his next boat appears to have been the *Little Flower* in the following year, in which another Kelvin 13–15hp unit was installed. In 1914 he launched two boats – the *Lady Charlotte*, CN174, and the *Lady Edith*, CN175 – both with the same 13–15hp units. By this time he had moved to a shed at the top of the Town Quay, where the Social Security building is now. Wylie, famous for his fast and regatta-winning skiffs such as *Sweet Home*, CN674, *Frigate Bird*, CN678, both built in 1903, and *Clemina*, CN139, built in 1901, continued building vessels after the First World War, although demand for the skiffs decreased after the hostilities. This is not to say there was no demand for new boats, but merely a reluctance on the part of the fishermen to invest in new boats. Even though the Fishery Board invited tenders from boatbuilders for the construction of a 'model Lochfyne motor skiff' in 1919, the tenders were too high at £1,100 to attract the fishermen's attentions, considering a new skiff cost about £140 at that time. Wylie's son, also Robert, took over the main work of the yard, and Wylie himself died in 1934 at the age of seventy-seven. The final boat launched from the yard was the fully-decked 50ft *Gratitude*, CN114, in 1936.

It is worth mentioning that the design gained favour in other parts of Scotland, most notably in the north-west. The Fishery Board reported in 1896 that 'skiffs of the Lochfyne build are considered the most suitable craft for local herring fishing' in Loch Broom, Sutherland. Many of the boats bought from Lochfyneside and the surrounding area were most likely to have been

Skiff at Portree, Isle of Skye.

trawl skiffs at a time when a huge upsurge in demand for the skiffs was occurring in the south. Several, however, were built in the north.

The *Queen Mary*, UL138, was built by Murdo MacDonald and his son Donald at Alligin, on the north side of Loch Torridon, in 1910 at a cost of £62. At 31ft overall – on a 22ft keel – she might not exactly be termed a Lochfyne skiff but was indeed similar in shape. Built using local larch and elm brought across the loch from the Ben-damph forest and cut in their own saw-pit, she was clinker-built. Belonging to John McKenzie of Gairloch, she was kept at Badachro where she fished for cod and herring in season. It is said that she sailed both to the Clyde and the Outer Hebrides for the herring. She later had a Kelvin 7–9hp unit fitted. Two further sister-boats, *Lady Marjorie* and *Isabella*, were also built at Alligin. All were of the Lochfyne layout, with a small forecastle, a hold and stern sheets. Notable differences were the fact that the floor in the stern sheets was a foot higher than in the hold and that there were two net platforms in the hold, one either side.

Three generations of the MacDonald family built many small *bata*-type craft for use in the fishery, some of which still exist. The last practising member, another Murdo, went out to Papua New Guinea to teach boatbuilding skills to the locals, before returning home and retiring. Today the *Queen Mary* is on display at the Gairloch Heritage Centre, alongside another small skiff. The boatbuilding shed is still at Alligin, albeit being used to sell fresh produce from nearby fields and hens! Another larger Lochfyne skiff was built for owners at Loch Kishorn, several miles to the south of Loch Torridon. The *Clan Gordon*, BRD121 (later UL240), came from Munro's yard in Ardrishaig in 1911, although there seems to be a bit of discrepancy here as Munro had already moved to Blairmore by that date. Another report says she was built by a yacht builder at Ardrishaig because the usual yard was too busy to accept the order! At 37ft overall, she was

Campbeltown fishermen aboard a skiff.

Typical pillbox wheelhouse fitted to skiffs after motorisation.

The 41ft *Britannia*. (Photo courtesy of William Cameron.)

perhaps smaller than some being built at the time. The *Clan McNab*, TT138, was built by David Munro of Blairmore in 1922.

Two other skiffs, the *Sireadh*, TT150, and the *Fairy Queen*, CN196, came from yards on the East Coast. The former was built by James Miller & Sons, St Monans in 1923, and the latter by James Nobles of Fraserburgh in 1926. All three of these skiffs (not the *Clan McNab*) are still afloat or being restored, a testament to the skill of their builders. The *Fairy Queen*, built to replace an earlier skiff of the same name, a model of which survives in the Campbeltown Museum, I found ashore at Kinvara, West Ireland, during a visit there in August 2007. The owner, Fred Moisy, had recently restored parts of the vessel and was hoping to put her back in the water within a matter of weeks.

It was Robert Robertson who again pioneered the new generation of boats after a trip to Norway having been impressed with the boats he had seen there. Returning home he instructed Glasgow naval architect W.G. McBride to design a vessel with a canoe stern, based on Norwegian types. Not for the first time were the vessels of Scandinavia to influence Scottish boats. McBride's plans were submitted to James Miller for tender and an order for two such vessels was placed. Thus *Falcon* and *Frigate Bird* arrived in Campbeltown in 1922, utterly unlike the skiffs. They retained their double-ended hull but there the similarity ended. They had canoe sterns and a rounded stem and very rounded forefoot, and were completely decked over. The keel sloped up towards the bow by only a few inches. In many respects, however, they can be seen as a development of the skiffs in that the hull was designed in a similar way with low freeboard to facilitate the use of the ring-net. The accommodation, with six bunks and a stove, was again situated in the forward end of the boat and the engines – each boat had two

Lochfyne skiff *Mary Graham* in Saddell, 1919, on regatta day. She was built by Fyfe of Port Bannatyne in 1901.

Hauling in a ring-net. (Photo courtesy of Angus Martin.)

Gleniffer 18–22hp units – in the stern. A lugsail was rigged and the rudder was hung externally and supported by a shoe that was an extension of the keel. A small pillbox wheelhouse provided shelter for the helmsman and the steering was by means of a wheel.

This innovation was soon copied aboard the skiffs. Both new boats were just over 50ft in overall length and had cost £1,277 14s each, excluding the cost of the nets and gear. Again there was a certain amount of scorn on the part of the fishermen who believed such innovations to be a waste of money, but Robertson soon proved the boats' worth. Although many accepted the need for fully-decked craft – three were ordered and delivered to Carradale owners in 1926 – they did not accept the larger size and the canoe stern. Robertson himself ordered a new boat from Miller's yard in the same year and the *Crimson Arrow*, although being built on similar lines to his previous two boats, was, indeed, 10ft smaller, since he found the extra freeboard a disadvantage to the men when basketing the herring aboard out of the net. Three years later, with the development of powered winches to aid the hauling in of the herring, he had the 46ft *Nil Desperandum* built by Miller, a boat notable by its forward wheelhouse, although five years later it was moved back aft.

In 1930 he sold his two original boats and had two new 52ft boats built – *Kestrel* and *Kittiwake*. By this time a transom-sterned boat, the *Unitas* from Saltcoats, had been adapted by having a canoe stern built on – the first Ayrshire boat to have such an arrangement. By 1933, thirteen new boats, all built on the East Coast of Scotland from the yards of Miller, Walter Reekie of St Monans, Weatherhead & Blackie of Cockenzie (previously William Weatherhead worked alone) and James Noble of Fraserburgh, were introduced in the Campbeltown and Carradale fleets while fourteen were added to the Ayrshire fleet at Dunure, Girvan and Ballantrae. The design had finally found favour and the demise of the older Lochfyne skiffs

Skiff *Ella*. (Photo courtesy of Mrs Margaret McBride Harvison.)

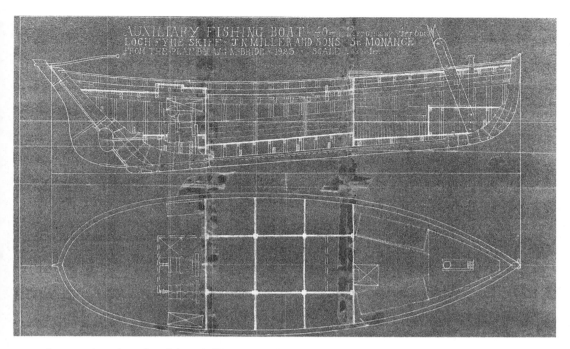

Construction plan of Lochfyne skiff by J.N. Miller & Sons of St Monance.

was now a certainty. Over the next few years many more ring-netters were built before war intervened once again.

Up to now most of the new boats on the Clyde were being built on the East Coast, although a few were emanating from Dickies of Tarbert and even fewer from the Fairlie yacht slip. That was until Alexander Noble moved to Girvan in 1946 and started up a boatbuilding yard. Originally from Fraserburgh where he had learned his trade, he moved to County Donegal in 1933 where he worked as the foreman, building Irish fishing vessels for the BIM (Irish Fisheries Department) before returning to the Clyde in 1937. There he worked in a yacht-building yard, engaged mostly in Admiralty work during the war. After commencing work on a patch of grass alongside the river at Girvan, the first boat was launched in 1947, followed by the first ring-net boat, the *Selina*, the following year. Over the next twenty-two years the yard built seventy-eight vessels, mostly fishing boats, with the last ring-netter, the *Alliance*, CN187, being built in 1974. However, with the demise of the ring-netting and the disappearance of the herring fleets, the end of fishing boatbuilding for the Clyde fleets quickly came about, although the yard still enjoys a prosperous time, building steel boats since 1984. The Campbeltown Shipyard Ltd also built over one hundred steel vessels between 1970 and 1997, although the vast majority went to owners outside the Clyde. Alex Noble also built the *Westerlea*, later known as *Huntress*, in 1971, but she was scrapped in 2002 as part of the European Union's decommissioning scheme, which is part of the disastrous EU fishing policy that has led to over-fishing, a quota system, and large-scale scrapping of perfectly seaworthy vessels, with no end in sight. Alex Noble died in 1993, a year before the hundredth boat was launched from the yard, which is now run by his sons, Peter and Jim.

Skiff built by McDonalds of Alligin, pictured lying at Alligin in 2002.

Skiffs at Campbeltown, 1922.

Queen May at Gareloch in 1991.

As a final reminder of the excellence of the Lochfyne skiffs, it is worth noting that a number of yachts were built according to similar designs. The yacht *May* was built by Alexander Robertson of Sandbank in 1902, and was perhaps the earliest of yacht builds; she sailed across the Atlantic. Others include *Kirsty*, *Rowan IV* and *Nighean Donn* which was last heard of in Stonehaven, although I think she has been sold on. More recently a small trawl skiff has been built in Tarbert with Heritage Lottery funding and there have been initial soundings for the building of a new yacht on skiff lines.

seven

A Story of *Perseverance*
CN152

The advert read, 'a lot of good Salt Herrings in Barrels, half barrels and firkins. Kippered daily from … '. Further down the page was a paragraph about the poor fishing that week and that there had only been sixteen trawls of herring landed, priced at 21s a box. The drift-netters had managed a shot of 300 herring, priced between 5s and 9s 9d.

I was reading the *Campbeltown Courier*, dated 29 June 1912, thanks to Murdo MacDonald, the chief archivist at the Argyll and Bute District Council offices in Lochgilphead. There was also a paragraph at the bottom of the local news section entitled 'New Fishing Skiff' which read:

> On Saturday there was launched from the boatbuilding yard of Robert Wylie a nicely modelled fishing skiff built to the order of a local firm, Messrs Mathieson, Wilkinson and McLean. The boat, which has the distinction of being the largest in the fleet, is carvel built, and has the following dimensions:- keel, 29ft; overall 40ft; beam 12ft 2in; depth, 7ft. She has been fitted with a 13.15 Kelvin motor, and has been named the 'Perseverance'. The skiff makes a fine addition to the Campbeltown fleet.

That was back in early 1992, two years after I had purchased the boat in Portugal and sailed her back to Campbeltown in 1991 where she was received with much rejoicing, and where I soon learned of the boat's registration number from the fishery office. After researching her history during those first two years, I had finally come across the missing piece for which I'd been searching: the very beginning of the story of *Perseverance*.

Even though the skiff – for she was a traditional Lochfyne skiff, albeit with a motor added – had been built for a firm, she was a dream-come-true for Archie 'Try' Mathieson, who had previously owned the clinker-built sailing skiff *Defender*, CN449, built by John Fyfe in Port Bannatyne in 1895. Mathieson's byname, 'Try', came from the name of the new boat, and, neighbouring with Duncan 'Captain' Wilkinson's *Ellen*, CN97, the two of them became known as the 'Desperates', renowned as they were for fishing in adverse weather when much of the fleet stayed in harbour.

On her maiden voyage in 1912, the *Perseverance* returned to Campbeltown loaded up to the 'bends' – that part of the vessel where the planking finishes just below the covering board.

Before sailing to the 'north herring' in the spring, the boat was hauled up and scrubbed and varnished, for she, like the majority of the fleet, had a bright work hull and no external paint save for her registration letters and numbers of CN152. Sailing through the Crinan Canal, the *Perseverance*, along with the rest of the fleet, sailed out to Mallaig and the fishing grounds amongst the Western Isles. One newspaper cutting I read told of the time Archie was fishing in the Kyle

Archie Mathieson, then skipper and owner of *Perseverance*, aboard just after the addition of her pillbox wheelhouse, *c.*1920.

of Uig, off Lewis, when he caught a boatload of fish before the weather deteriorated to such an extent that he had to seek shelter, such was the weight of fish aboard. He put into the village of Hacklete, where amazed villagers were told to help themselves to the fish in order to lighten the load and enable him to sail back to Mallaig.

Another time the fleet was sheltering from a storm in the Island of Canna when one of the islanders was taken ill and a doctor from Mallaig urgently needed. The fishermen were asked if anyone would sail over to collect him and Archie volunteered, setting off in horrendous conditions to return several hours later with the doctor. Much of this information came from Mary Smith, one of Archie's daughters who lived in nearby Machrihanish. Another daughter, Kate MacWilliam, living in Rothesay, also filled in some of the history of the boat. It was thus with great joy that we held a party on board the boat on 21 June 1992, eighty years to the day that the boat had been launched. The party was attended by Kate, Mary, her husband Hughie and brother Alex, many older fishermen and Angus Martin, author of *The Ring-Net Fishermen*, a book that had given me an initial insight into the world of the Lochfyne skiffs. Neil MacDougall, grandson of Matthew MacDougall, the boatbuilder of Carradale, was also present and recounted tales of the times he remembered the boat working from Carradale. He added that, from a boatbuilder's point of view, he thought she was the finest conversion he had ever seen. Both Mary and Kate were emotional being aboard the boat after so many years. They spoke of the importance of the boat as a means of feeding the family, and how their father, who died in 1955, had been justly proud of it and had kept it in the finest condition.

The Clyde Fishermen's Association. Archie Mathieson is in the centre, seated.

Perseverance off the Isle of Wight. (Photo courtesy of C. Laity.)

Perseverance off Porthleven, *c.*1950. (Photo courtesy of C. Laity.)

Originally fitted with the 13.15hp petrol/paraffin Kelvin, Archie changed this in about 1928 for a more powerful engine. Keeping to the Kelvin name, he chose a sleeve-valve engine, type C2 of 30hp. With this, she became a fast boat and a berth upon the *Perseverance* was one of the most sought-after positions, thus the saying, 'the *Perseverance* just outside, the fastest sleeve-valve in the Clyde'. Archie was renowned as a fair skipper, sharing the fish money so that each crew member, including himself and the boat, received one share, with the boy and engine receiving a half share each. When receipts were poor, he refused to take a share for the boat or the engine.

Later on, the exact date being unclear, he added a small wheelhouse and wheeled steering. During the Second World War he continued fishing, despite being in his seventies, hoping that his son would carry on the family tradition, although sadly he returned from the war disabled. In 1944 he changed the engine once again and fitted a Kelvin J4 diesel of 44hp, the same engine that was in her when I bought her in 1990. The *Perseverance*, unlike many other converted skiffs, never had a wing engine.

In 1946, after over thirty years of excellent service, Archie sold the *Perseverance* to Anthony Watkins, who used her for catching basking sharks between 1946 and '49 alongside two other local boats, the *Paragon* and *Dusky Maid*. His story is told in *The Sea My Hunting Ground*, written by Watkins and published in 1958, three years after Archie Mathieson died.

In 1949 the boat was sold to Charlie and Bill Laity of Porthleven, Cornwall, who took her over in Tarbert and sailed her south, registering her in Penzance as PZ1. During the summer

95

The *Perseverance* just outside the mouth of the Clyde.

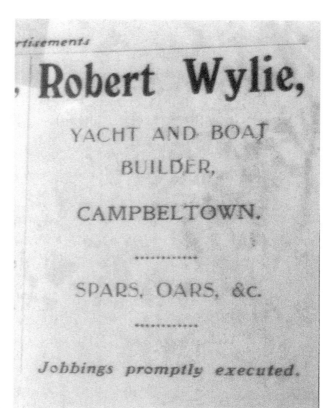

Advert for Wylie's yard.

Perseverance at Lagos, Portugal 1990.

Perseverance soon after her launch in 1912.

they used her for line fishing, landing into Newlyn, and drift-netting off Plymouth in the winter. Bill later sold out to Charlie, who then refitted the Kelvin to the front of the boat and converted the old engine room into accommodation, with fish and net rooms between, an arrangement preferred by many of the Cornish fishermen. In 1952 the boat was sold to Skip Wallis of Falmouth, who bought her to sail a crew of Sea Cadets up the river Thames for the Queen's Coronation, although he never succeeded in doing this. He subsequently used the *Perseverance* to teach navigation and seamanship to the Sea Cadets, keeping her moored on Customs Quay, Falmouth, the only person allowed to do so as he had been there longer than the present regulations which forbid permanent berthing. Skip sold her in 1958 and over the next ten years she went through a succession of owners, mainly being used as a houseboat in Sailors Creek, where Chris Mitchell found and purchased her in 1968. Between 1973 and '75, Chris undertook a full rebuild of the boat on Ponsharden Beach replacing rotten frames, the entire elm keel, replacing almost three quarters of the hull and converting the inside for living aboard. He managed to buy back the Kelvin J4 which had been sold off to Ron Twydle of Falmouth during her stint as a houseboat, and replaced it in the after end of the boat. Furthermore, he rigged her as a gaff ketch, enabling her to sail once again. Chris then sailed with his family to Norway, back via Germany and Holland, and then departed for France, Spain and finally Portugal, where I found her for sale in 1990.

I owned the fine vessel for five years, sailing her mainly around Scotland, eventually returning her to my home in Wales, via the Isle of Man. Then, unfortunately, I sold her in May 1995 to two Irish owners intent on sailing away to the Mediterranean for a year or two. Six months later I heard that they had collided with something 200 miles off the Portuguese coast and that the boat had sunk in minutes, something I found very strange considering the

Crew aboard *Perseverance*, Archie Mathieson in the centre, *c.*1915.

Perseverance out of the water, 1993.

Perseverance, pictured with the author standing. Note bulwarks built up especially at the stern. She was converted to a gaff ketch around 1980, when she was rebuilt by Chris Mitchell of Falmouth.

Above and below: Under reconstruction on the beach at Ponsharden, Falmouth, 1972-75. (Photos courtesy of Chris Mitchell.)

Under reconstruction on the beach at Ponsharden, Falmouth, 1972-75. (Photo courtesy of Chris Mitchell.)

Perseverance in Sailor's Creek, late 1960s, when being used as a houseboat. (Photo by Chris Mitchell)

Chris Mitchell. (Photo by Chris Mitchell)

In Falmouth shipyard. (Photo courtesy of Chris Mitchell.)

The Kelvin J4 during rebuild. (Photo courtesy of Chris Mitchell.)

strength of the hull and the watertight bulkheads incorporated by Chris Mitchell when he rebuilt her.

Everything, everybody, needs an epitaph. Reading Alistair Maclean's *The Dileas* I found a passage relevant to the skiffs. Although I cannot remember what the book is about, I recently came across two excerpts I'd noted down at the time. He wrote, 'when Campbell of Ardrishaig built a Loch Fyner, the timbers came out of the heart of the oak'. This could certainly apply to the *Perseverance*, and many other skiffs as well as any other boat. For a fitting epitaph, though, I prefer his later words, 'then we came tearing down the sound, steady as a rock – for in a heavy stern sea there's no boat the equal of a Loch Fyner'.

eight

Two Surviving Skiffs –
Sireadh and the *Clan Gordon*

Sireadh of Minard

Ordered from the yard of James Miller of St Monans, her keel was laid on 1 June 1923 and the boat delivered three months later for a total cost of £751 3s. Rigged with one standing lug and a Kelvin 13.15hp engine, she had been designed by William McBride of Glasgow, the designer of *Falcon* and *Frigate Bird*, and presumably built at the same yard because of the designer's wishes, for *Sireadh* – Gaelic for 'seeker' – was the only Lochfyne skiff ever built by Miller. Her owners, Duncan and Alex Munro, Robert McGilp and James Turner, were all fishermen from Minard, in the upper reaches of Loch Fyne. She was registered as TT150 and neighboured alongside the *Clan McNab*, TT138, built in 1922. Both boats were amongst the largest in the fleet, the *Sireadh* measuring 40ft overall on a 29ft 6in keel, while the *Clan McNab* was the largest skiff ever built at 42ft 8in on a 31ft keel.

That the fishermen of the upper loch were successful at fishing is reflected in the large family houses they built alongside the loch in the late 1800s. Jubilee Villa was built by Alex Munro's father Robert in 1888, and the family still retains ownership of the house. I'm told that the piano was delivered aboard the *Sireadh*.

There were four other large skiffs working out of Minard in the first decade or two of the twentieth century: *Britannia*, TT81 (probably previously TT69, AG239, built by J. Fyfe in 1893); *Treasure*, TT316, built by J. Fyfe in 1909; *Ladye*, TT221, previously 281AG and built by D. McTavish in 1896; and *Lily*, TT152, previously AG252, built by A. Munro in 1894, as well as the smaller boats *Snipe, Jessie* and *Marsealladh*. The two previous skiffs, *Lady Campbell*, TT230, AG139, built by J. Fyfe in 1890, and *Merrily*, TT224, were sold to finance the new boats, *Lady Campbell* becoming BA309 in 1923.

Both *Sireadh* and *Clan McNab* had wheelhouses added, the former in the late 1920s and the latter in 1934. Fishing was poor by that time and wages as low as £35 a year were common, whereas a man could earn £1 a week in the woods above Minard. Consequently many stopped fishing altogether so that only these two boats remained fishing into the 1930s. *Sireadh* was eventually sold in 1938 followed by the *Clan McNab* the year after.

Sireadh was purchased by a Mr Wilson from Belfast who converted her into a pleasure yacht. Ten years later he changed her name to *Golden Plover*. She was sold again in 1950 and again in 1952. A Gardner engine was fitted in 1953, before she passed through the hands of several owners in 1954, 1959, 1962 and 1968, by which time she was in Bridlington. The new owners, a one-legged retired Lt-Col and his wife, sailed her to Cyprus and later voyaged around Greece, the

Sireadh out of the water at Burlsedon, 2000.

Sireadh's extreme raking stern post, 2000.

Sireadh on the River Hamble, *c.*1980.

Sireadh loading up passengers for the annual Sunday School trip. Alexander Munro is standing amidships with the peaked cap. Willie Munro (his son) is ferrying passengers out in the rowing boat. Photo taken at the pier in front of Jubilee. (Photo courtesy of Willie Crawford.)

Adriatic, the Turkish archipelago, Lebanon and Israel. They decided to sell in 1976, at which time she was returned to the river Hamble before being taken out of the water at Moody's Yard at Lower Swanwick. In 1978 she was purchased by Paul and Janet Baker who had lain alongside her on their Falmouth oyster boat and dreamed of owning her to sail around the world. When their boat was later stolen, and the owners of *Golden Plover* about to depart to the States, they used their insurance money to buy her. Seven years of hard work, much rebuilding, re-rigging and fitting-out followed. At the same time they researched the boat's history and renamed her *Sireadh*. Their maiden voyage was to the Douarnenez festival in 1988. Two years later, they sailed to the Mediterranean via the French canals, where they cruised the Balearic Islands, the Spanish coast, Gibraltar and Morocco, before arriving in the Canary Islands. Then, in 1993, after finding water a foot deep in the cabin while on passage, they rushed to Tenerife to haul out, only to discover that toredo worm had eaten the garboards. After replacing them, they completed their navigation of Madeira and the Azores, before arriving back in the Solent in 1995. *Sireadh* lay in the river Hamble for several years until sinking, upon which she was taken ashore and bought by a local man before being sold to a new owner in Dartmouth where she is currently experiencing a full refit.

Clan Gordon of Kishorn

Built in 1911 at Ardrishaig, her original registration was BRD121 and she was worked by the Gordon family in the Kyle District. Not much is known about her earlier history but she was re-registered as UL240 in 1943 and then sold in 1946 to a Mr Watson who lived at Gareloch, before being sold on his death to the Northern Lighthouse Board in 1958. Based in Portree, she was used as a vessel to service the lighthouse on Rona, taking lighthouse keepers out and supplying their needs. Skippered by Charlie MacLeod, her crew consisted of his brother and one other person. Charlie remembers the 'wee cockpit' behind a crutch for supporting the mast which was suspended from a pulley, enabling a piece of canvas to be raised to chin height affording a limited protection to the helmsman. Later a wheelhouse was added.

Although she had a 13.15hp Kelvin when built, this had been replaced with a Kelvin-Ricardo four-cylinder 30.36hp petrol/paraffin. She was withdrawn from service in December 1964 because of her state and sold to Jon Corrigan of Portree who sold her a few months later to Leo Clegg, the coxswain of the Aberdeen Lifeboat. Once again details of her life become unclear for Clegg died and an Albert Bird owned the boat for a while. Then Pip Hills found her in a shed in 1988 somewhere near Brechin, after seeing her afloat in Tayport a few years before. According to Hills, he'd heard about the boat in the pub and found the owner who had a sort of fishing tackle and Nazi memorabilia shop. It seems the fellow had an almost ruined castle in which he was living and where he intended to restore the boat. He wanted £800 for the boat, but Hills bought it for something less. Once he got it to Granton, Hills took off the deck which was entirely rotten, replaced much of the frames and planking above the waterline, scarped a piece into the stem, replaced new deck timbers and planks and got the Kelvin J4 which was aboard her working. He rigged her with a standing lug and foresail so that, for the first time in many years, a traditionally rigged skiff was able to sail again. I sailed aboard the boat for a brief foray around the Firth of Forth in 2002, a couple of years or so before he sold her to James McGregor. He sailed her to Ullapool where he now moors her, and where I last saw her in 2005, looking wonderful with her varnished hull and original rig.

Sireadh loaded with family treasures, *c*.1930.

Sireadh ready for refit, Hamble, *c*.2000.

Above: Clan Gordon at Granton in 2001.

Right: Clan Gordon on Loch Broom in 2002.

Clan Gordon, Ullapool, 2002.

Opposite above: Clan Gordon, Ullapool, 2002. (Photo courtesy of Charles Mcleod.)

Opposite below: Clan Gordon by pier at Roma Lighthouse, *c.*1950. (Photo courtesy of Charles McLeod.)

Clan Gordon sailing in 1999.

Clan Gordon.

nine

Motorised Ringers –
A Few Examples

Glen Carradale, CN253 (48.1ft)

Built in 1933 by Walter Reekie, St Monans, for Lawrence McBride, she had a Kelvin 44hp aboard. In 1941 the ownership passed to Alexander Sharp McBride and the engine was replaced with a Kelvin 66hp in 1947. She neighboured the *Fairy Queen*, CN128, *Nobles Again*, CN37, and *Golden Fleece*, CN170. In 1955 she was sold to Alasdair Gibson of Lochbuie, Mull, and the registration was cancelled in 1962.

What happened next is unclear, although she didn't fish. Sometime in the later 1980s she appeared at Lochaline, where it seems she was finally abandoned alongside the old jetty at the top of the loch. Over the next few years or so she gradually fell apart until the hull collapsed and split in two. In 2001 both the stem and sternpost were lying flat, although the hull planking still retained some degree of shape, while the rudder and Kelvin stern tube still remained. The deck was lying atop the beach in two sections. During a field trip with other members of the Scottish Institute of Maritime Studies at St Andrews University, I undertook a survey of the wreck site and drew up the plan below.

Village Maid II, TT25 (58.55ft)

Built by Alexander Noble & Sons in Girvan in 1961 for Willie and Neil Jackson, she was a descendant of the first of her type – the 58ft *Saffron*, BA182, built for the McCrindle family in 1951. The *Village Maid II* remained fishing out of Tarbert until 1990. She was the first Tarbert boat to be fitted with an inflatable liferaft, stored on the wheelhouse roof. Her original engine was a Gardner 8L3B, 152hp, but this was changed for a Volvo Penta 270hp unit when she was pair-trawling. In 1990 she was sold to Robert Summers of Mallaig and registered as OB154. She was decommissioned in 1994 and scrapped.

Watchful, BA124 (56ft)

Built by Weatherhead & Blackie of Port Seton in 1959, she neighboured with the *Wisteria* under the ownership of Matt Sloan of the Maidens, Ayrshire. When Matt came ashore in 1971 she was sold in the following year to David and John Morrison of Scalpay, Harris, and renamed *Majestic*,

Motor ringer *Glen Carradale*.

Glen Carradale (CN253) was built in 1933 and is pictured here around 1979. She fell apart in the 1980s in Lochaline, and her remains still lie on the beach there.

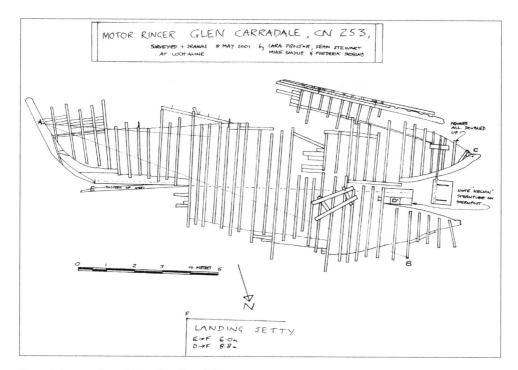

Plan of the remains of the *Glen Carradale*.

Villiage Maid II.

The *Watchful*.

The ring-netters *Watchful* on left and *Wisteria* on right.

The *Watchful* ashore at Ayr, 1997.

SY137. She was sold again in 1983 to Denis Meenan of Campbeltown and renamed *Stella Maris*, CN158. She was decommissioned in 1994 and put ashore at Ayr as an exhibit, thanks to the efforts of Andy Alexander, who crewed aboard her while she fished from the Maidens, and later became a skipper-owner. Her current state is unknown.

Minnie McLean, OB80 (54.6ft)

Another Weatherhead & Blackie boat – considered the best by many Ayrshire men – built in 1962 for Jimmy MacLean of Mallaig. She was sold in 1977 to new owner Alexander MacArthur, Balemartine, and renamed *Christina*. In 1999 she was sold to Leslie Morrish as one of three boats to be sailed across to Honduras carrying aid after the devastating hurricane there. Although *Christina* sailed to Plymouth in January 2000, with the author aboard, the project never succeeded and the boat was refitted on the river Lyner where she remains today.

Pathfinder, BA252 (59.6ft)

Built by Alexander Nobles of Girvan in 1964 for Bert Andrews of the Maidens, as a seine-netter/ring-netter, she neighboured *Ocean Gem*, BA265. She became OB181 in 1973 and by 2005 was owned by Hakin Seafoods of Ayr.

The 18m *Pathfinder* (BA252), built in Girvan in 1964.

Christina ex-Minnie McLean in 1998.

Nulli Secundus at Campbeltown. (Photo courtesy of Angus Martin.)

Fair Morn, BA295 (61.6ft)

Built in 1966 as a dual-purpose ring-netter by Herd & Mackenzie of Buckie for Alex Munro of Dunure, she neighboured *New Dawn*, BA18. She was later sold to Robert and Winifred M. Palmer of Portavogie. In 1983 she moved to the Moray Firth, being registered as INS319, and the following year she was renamed as the *Anna Bhan*. She was decommissioned in 1994.

Falcon, CN97 (50.2ft)

Built by James Miller & Sons in 1922 for Robert 'Hoodie' Robertson and designed by W.G. McBride, she was the prototype for the canoe-sterned ring-net boat. She was fitted with two Gleniffer 18–22hp engines. She was subsequently sold to Dan Conley in 1930, a former partner in Robertson's company.

Golden West, BA52 (48.1ft)

Built by Weatherhead and Blackie, Cockenzie, in 1926 for the McCrindle Brothers of the Maidens, and skippered by Thomas 'Wee Tam' McCrindle, she neighboured *Consort* and *Golden*

Fair Morn, representing the dual-purpose ring-netter. (Photo courtesy of Angus Martin.)

The *Falcon*. (Photo courtesy of Angus Martin.)

Carradale Pier.

Sheaf, BA195. She became WK396, A340 and latterly LK458, when she fished out of Hamnavoe in Shetland until 1976.

Nulli Secundus, CN246 (48ft)

Built by Walter Reekie of St Monans in 1932 for Robert Robertson, John Short and John Wareham, she was sold on 11 September 1937 to James Tod of Carradale and skippered by George Ritchie. She was sold again the following year to the McDougalls of Tarbert, and renamed *Mairearad*, TT113. She neighboured with *Fionnaghal*, TT65. In 1957 she was sold to Ireland and renamed the *Irish Rose*. Unconfirmed reports suggest she sank off Majorca after a gas bottle exploded.

Appendix I

Scottish Fishing Boats from around the Coast

The West Coast

OBAN SKIFF – double-ender, single lug-sailed vessel in use in the Inner Hebrides

LARGS SKIFF – double-ender for inner part of the Firth of Clyde, similar to the oban skiff

GIRVAN SKIFF – a smaller version of the nabbie that worked in the outer reaches of the Clyde

LOCH FYNE LINE BOAT – a small open boat used for long-lining within the reaches of Upper Loch Fyne which is similar to, if not the same as, the wherries

PORTPATRICK LINE BOAT – typical two-masted boat working in the North Channel for whitefish

SOLWAY FIRTH OR ANNAN SKIFF – a salmon boat working the whammel-net in the Solway Firth

BATA – Gaelic term for 'boat' used for fishing, ferrying and general use

GRIMSAY BOAT – lobster boat from the Stewart family from Grimsay used for creeling off the Monach Isles

BARRA LINE BOAT – similar type used for setting long-lines from Barra

NESS SGOTH – large beach boat used for fishing long-lines out of Ness in the north of the Isle of Lewis

GREENIE – skiff from around Greencastle, Northern Ireland, favoured by line fishermen from Islay and the Campbeltown area

The Northern Isles

SIXAREEN – the deep-sea 'haaf' fishery double-ender sailed out to long-line in deep water from Shetland

FOUREEN – a smaller version of the sixareen originally with four oars

NESS YOAL – a particular double-ender in use around the tidal waters of the south of Shetland

FAIR ISLE SKIFF – skiff developed in Fair Isle rigged with single squaresail

NORTH ORKNEY YOLE – two-masted standing lug-rigged double-ender

SOUTH ORKNEY YOLE – two-masted sprit-rigged double-ender

WHILLY BOAT – small fishing and general purpose boat from Orkney

STROMA YOLE – a fuller version of the Orkney yoles

WESTRAY SKIFF – a smaller single-masted lug-rigged skiff

HERRING YAWL – a dandy-rigged fifie built in both Shetland and Orkney

The East Coast

SCAFFIE – lug-rigged two-master from Wick with sloping sternpost and shallow forefoot

WICK YOLE – similar to those from Stroma, even said to have been introduced from there

FIFIE – large, deep double-ender with upright stem and stern from south of the Moray Firth, rigged with two huge dipping lugs

BAULDIE – a smaller version of the fifie introduced for long-lining and named after the Italian patriot Garibaldi

FIFIE YAWL– the tiniest version of the fifie

ZULU – a hybrid between the fifie and scaffie, fast and the elite of British fishing craft, characterised by its heavily sloping sternpost

½-ZULU – intermediate sized zulu with less sloping sternpost for motor installing

ZULU SKIFF – a much smaller single-masted version of the latter

FRASERBURGH YOLE – small single-masted boat built in Fraserburgh in the early years of the twentieth century

SALMON COBLE – flat-bottomed open boat for servicing salmon nets close to the shore, characterised by its up-turned stem

CREEL BOAT – small creel boat built on the Fife coast (Millers of St Monans and Smith & Hutton of Anstruther) for lobster and crab fishing

Note: Currachs and coracles, skin boats generally associated with Ireland and Wales, were in use in parts of Scotland, as were log boats and other early forms of watercraft, but have not been included here

Above: Two small Orkney yoles in the foreground and the Kirkwall–registered Firthie (or Fifie) *Rose* of Holm.

Left: The Shetland herring boat *Swan*.

The Old Pier, Kyleakin, Skye.

Ness Sgoth.

Barra boat.

Landing the catch at Ullapool.

Zulus and Fifies.

Scottish East Coast boats.

Tommy Isbister of Shetland in his ness yoal that he built.

Salmon coble fishermen with seire net.

Fifie.

The last sailing drifter in the Outer Hebrides – the small zulu *Muirneag*, SY436, which fished until 1945 and was subsequently chopped up and used as fencing posts – the ultimate fate of many ex-working crafts.

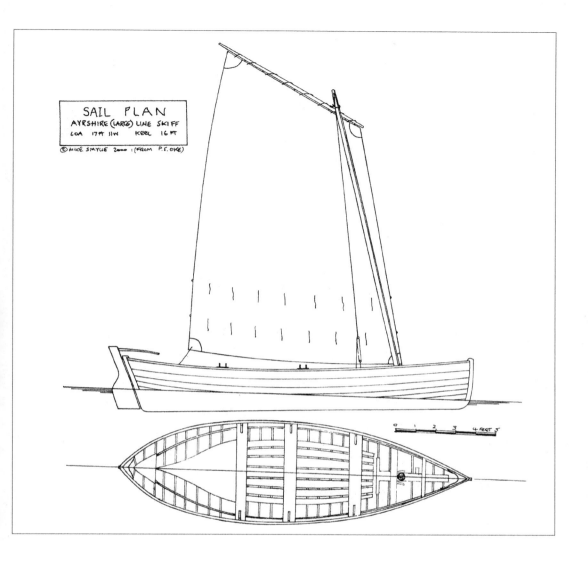

SAIL PLAN
AYRSHIRE (LARGE) LINE SKIFF
LOA 17FT 11W   KEEL 16 FT
© MIKE SMYLIE 2000 : (FROM P.J. OKE)

0 1 2 3 4 FEET 5

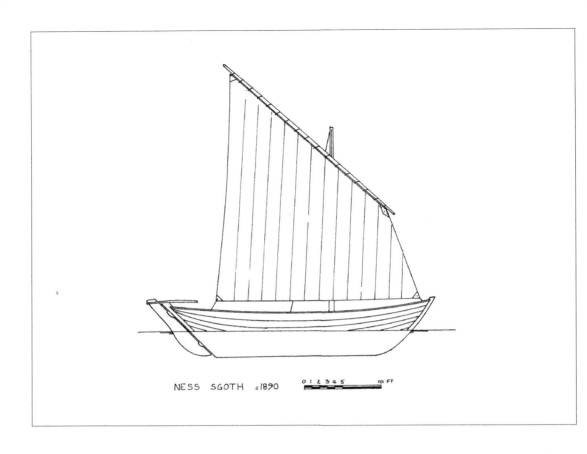

NESS SGOTH c1890

0 1 2 3 4 5   10 FT

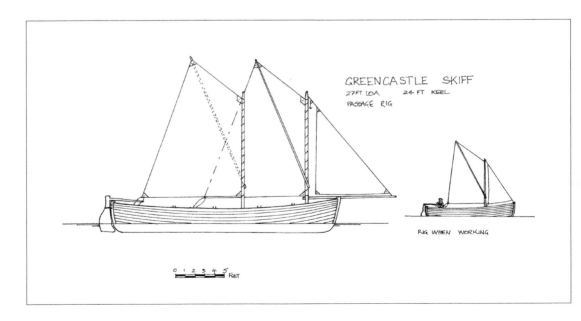

GREENCASTLE SKIFF
27 FT LOA.   24 FT KEEL
PASSAGE RIG

RIG WHEN WORKING

0 1 2 3 4 5 FEET

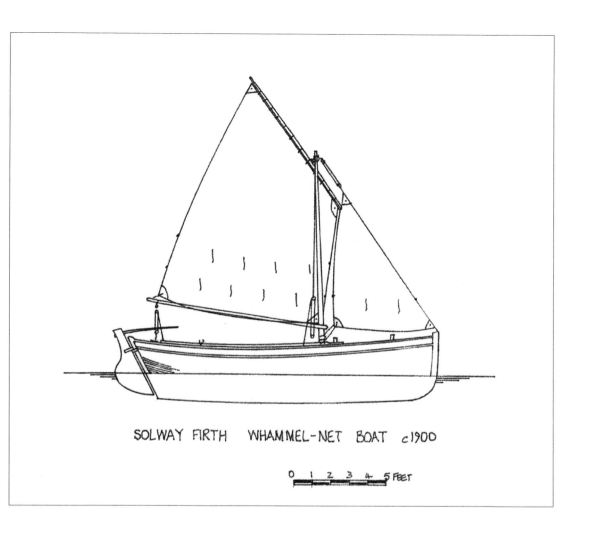

SOLWAY FIRTH   WHAMMEL-NET BOAT c 1900

0 1 2 3 4 5 FEET

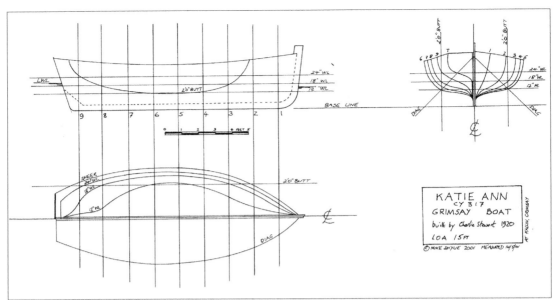

KATIE ANN
CY 317
GRIMSAY BOAT
built by Charlie Stewart 1920
LOA 15 FT
© MIKE SMYLIE 2001 MEASURED 14/9/01
AT KALLIN, GRIMSAY

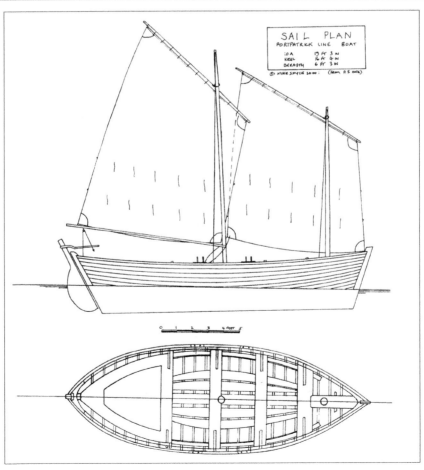

SAIL PLAN
PORTPATRICK LINE BOAT
LOA   19 FT 3 IN
KEEL   16 FT 4 IN
BREADTH   6 FT 3 IN
© MIKE SMYLIE 2000 :   (FROM P.S OKES)

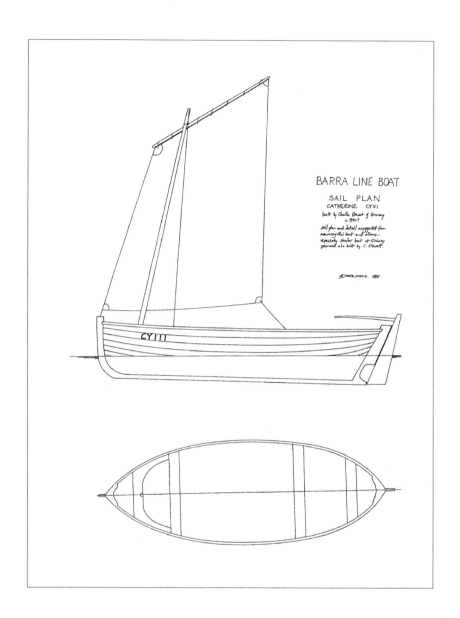

BARRA LINE BOAT

SAIL PLAN
CATHERINE CYIII

built by Charlie Stewart of Grimsay
c. 1910?

sail plan and detail copyright from
measuring this boat and others —
especially similar boat at Grimsay
preserved also built by C. Stewart.

CYIII

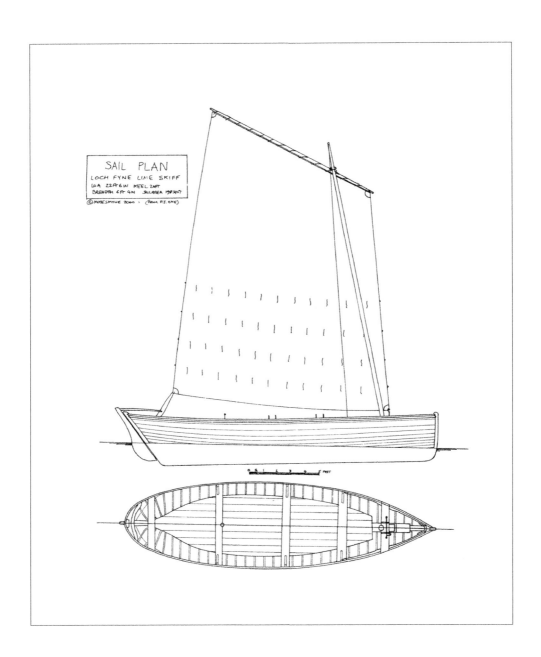

SAIL PLAN
LOCH FYNE LIME SKIFF
LOA 22FT 6IN   KEEL 2OFT
BREADTH 6FT 9IN   SAIL AREA 198 SQ FT
© MIKE SMYLIE 2000 ; (FROM P.J. OKE)

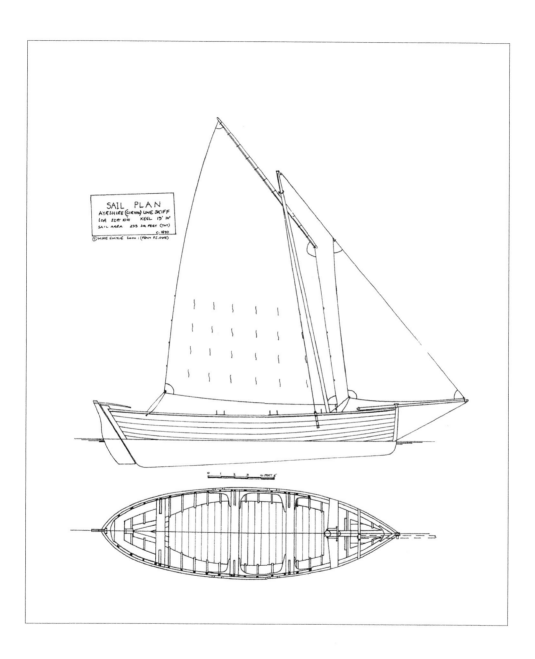

SAIL PLAN
AYRSHIRE (GIRVAN) LINE SKIFF
LOA 22 FT 10 IN   KEEL 15' 10"
SAIL AREA 233 SQ FEET (TOT)
C. 1890
© MIKE SMYLIE 2000 : (FROM R.S. OLVER)

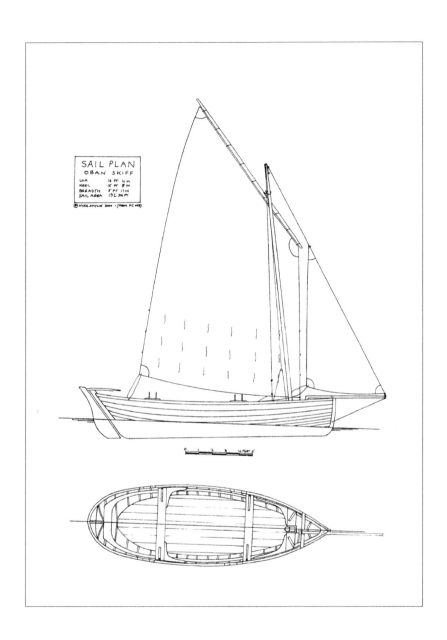

SAIL PLAN
OBAN SKIFF
LOA   18 FT 4 IN
KEEL   15 FT 8 IN
BREADTH   5 FT 11 IN
SAIL AREA 192 SQ FT

© IAIN OUGHTRED 2000 · (FROM F.J. M3)

0 1 2 3 4 FEET

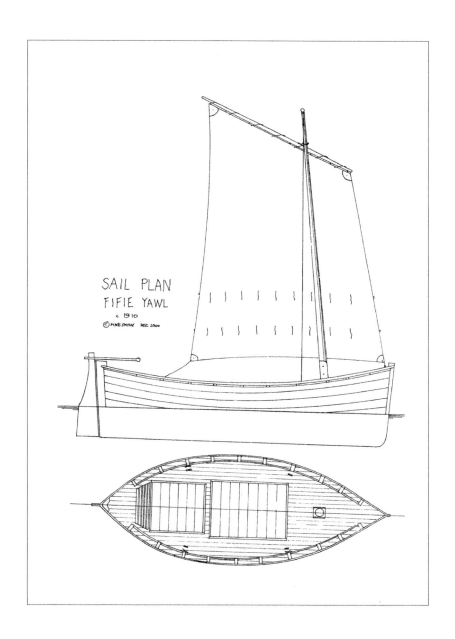

SAIL PLAN
FIFIE YAWL
c 1910
© MIKE SMYLIE DEZ 2000

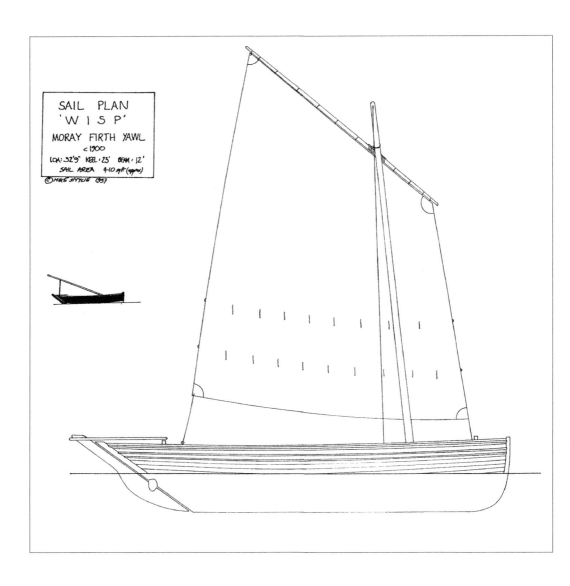

SAIL PLAN
'W I S P'
MORAY FIRTH YAWL
c 1900
LOA: 32'9" KEEL: 23' BEAM: 12'
SAIL AREA 410 ft² (approx)
© MIKE SMYLIE 1997

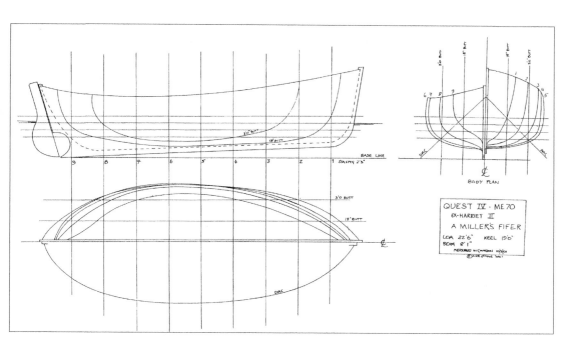

QUEST IV - ME 70
EX-HARRIET II
A MILLER'S FIFER
LOA 22'6"   KEEL 19'0"
BEAM 8'1"

BODY PLAN

BASE LINE

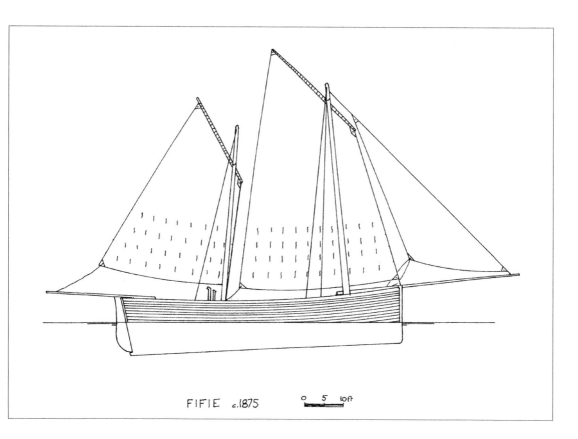

FIFIE c.1875   0   5   10ft

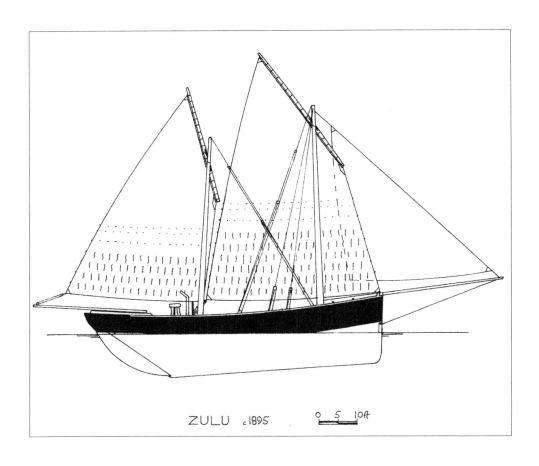

ZULU c1895

0   5   10A

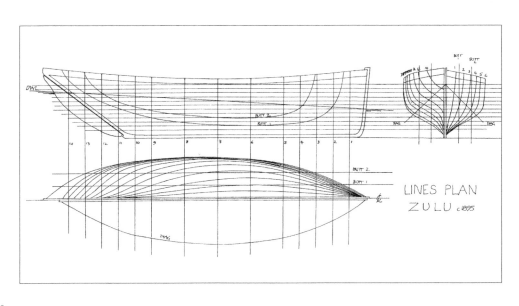

LINES PLAN
ZULU c1895

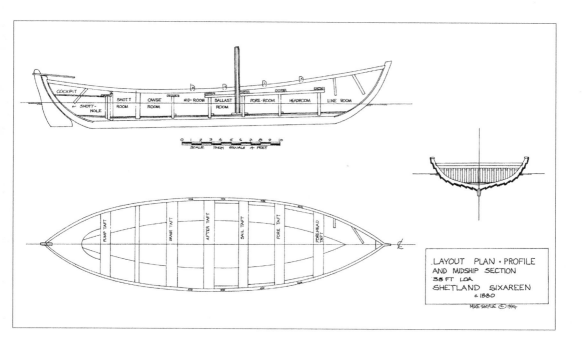

COCKPIT

or SHOTT-HOLE

SHOTT ROOM | OWISE ROOM | MID-ROOM | BALLAST ROOM | FORE-ROOM | HEADROOM | LINE ROOM

0 1 2 3 4 5 6 7 8 9 10
SCALE 1 INCH EQUALS 4 FEET

PUMP TAFT | SKAR TAFT | AFTER TAFT | SAIL TAFT | FORE TAFT | FOREHEAD TAFT

LAYOUT PLAN · PROFILE
AND MIDSHIP SECTION
38 FT LOA
SHETLAND SIXAREEN
c 1880

MIKE SMYLIE © 1994

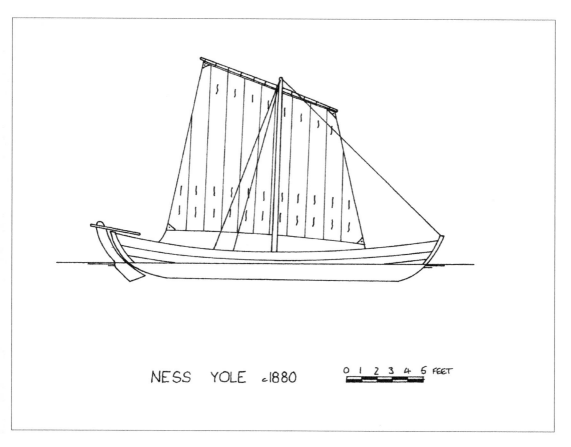

NESS YOLE c1880

0 1 2 3 4 5 FEET

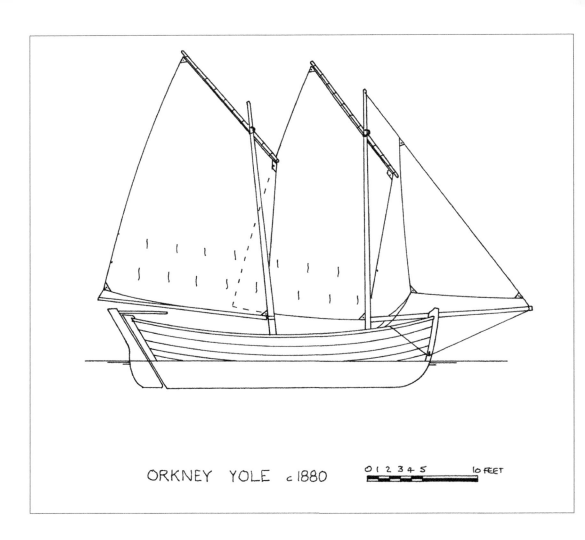

ORKNEY YOLE c 1880

0 1 2 3 4 5   10 FEET

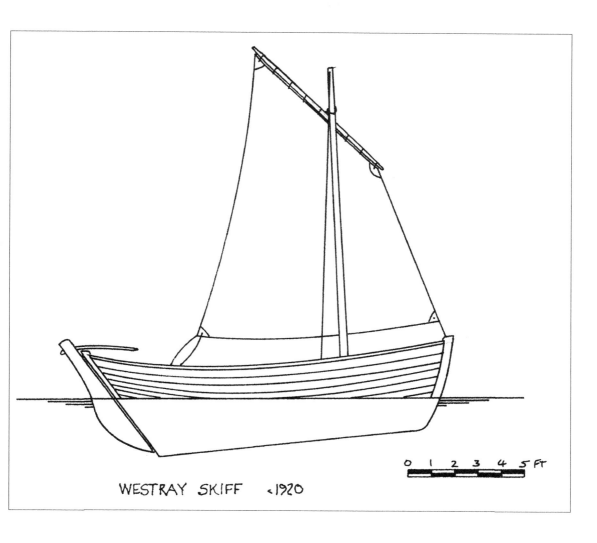

WESTRAY SKIFF c1920

0 1 2 3 4 5 Ft

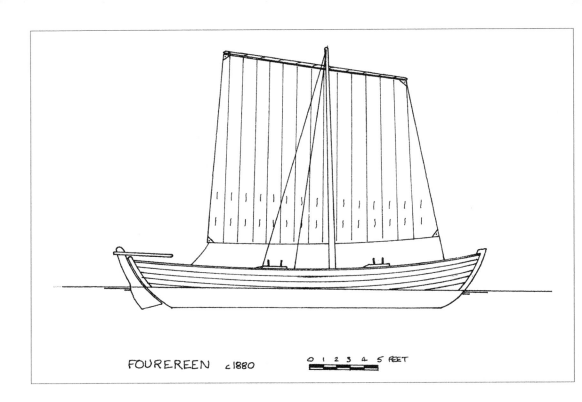

FOURER EEN c 1880

0 1 2 3 4 5 FEET

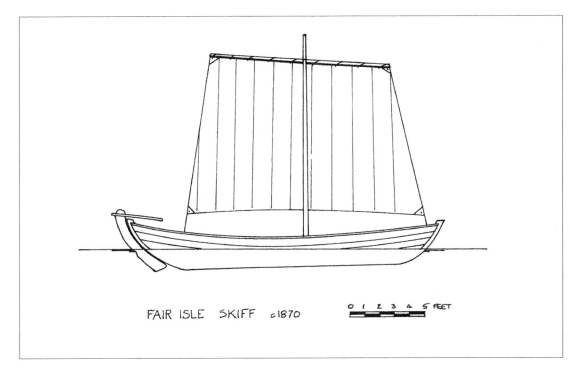

FAIR ISLE SKIFF c 1870

0 1 2 3 4 5 FEET

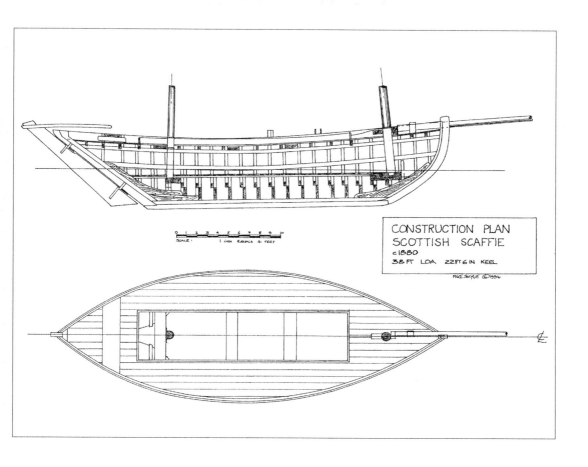

SCALE: 0 1 2 3 4 5 6 7 8 9 10   1 INCH EQUALS 4 FEET

CONSTRUCTION PLAN
SCOTTISH SCAFFIE
c1880
38 FT LOA 22 FT 6 IN KEEL

MIKE SMYLIE ©1994

Appendix II

Builders of Lochfyne Skiffs

Key to map

1. Campbeltown Lachie Lang 1883
   John Wardrope 1883
   Robert Wylie 1893–1934?
2. Carradale Matthew McDougal
   Donald Brown (Torrisdale) 1886
3. Tarbert Alexander & Duncan McTavish 1881–*c.*1900
   A. Henderson 1884–1905
   Dugald Henderson 1886–1905
   James Henderson 1886–1905
   Archibald Leitch 1885–1903
   Archibald Dickie 1904, became A.M. Dickie & Sons in 1912
   W. McMillan 1913
   Thomas Fyfe 1902
4. Ardrishaig James McLean 1882–1889, taken over by Munro's below
   A. Munro 1892–1913
   R. Munro 1897
   William Munro 1908
   Robert Fyfe 1902–09
   Archibald McCallum 1882–87
   John McEwan 1888
   Walker
5. Crinan Ferry Angus McLachlan 1888
6. Oban Donald McDonald
7. Jura John McDougal
   Donald Rankin (Ardlussa)
8. Inveraray A. & D. Munro 1892–1908, moved to Blairmore 1908–23
9. Tignabruich Archibald Smith 1905
10. Rothesay James Fyfe (Port Bannatyne) 1888–1923
    McLea, yard closed in 1880
    Ardmaleish
    Black
11. Dunoon Turner & Young

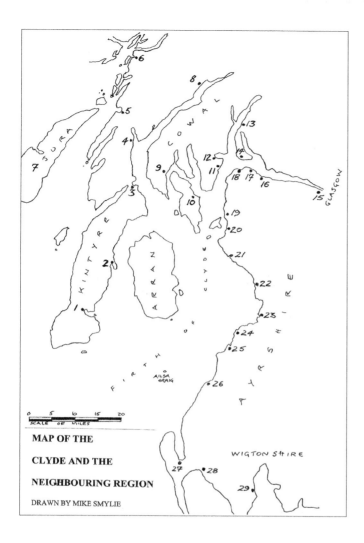

MAP OF THE

CLYDE AND THE

NEIGHBOURING REGION

DRAWN BY MIKE SMYLIE

12. Holy Loch Morris & Lorimer 1912
    Ewing & George McGruer 1900
13. Portincaple Walter Allison 1923
14. Kilcreggan Andrew McLaren 1900
    Archie McKellar 1908
15. Paisley Daniel Fyfe, moved to Tarbert between 1887 and 1903
16. Port Glasgow James McKenzie 1894
17. Greenock John McLeod 1881
    Peter Hanson 1920
18. Gourock John Barr
    James Adam 1870s
19. Largs John Ninian 1893
20. Fairlie William Fife c.1800–1902

J.Fyfe 1882

Hugh Boag, late 1860s–93

21. Ardrossan John Thomson 1899–1919
22. Troon Ailsa Shipyard *c.*1890, moved to Girvan
23. Ayr Archibald Boyd
24. Dunure Eaglesome 1901

     John Munro 1901

     Hugh Edgar

     William Harbison
25. Maidens Culzean Shipbuilding & Engineering Co. *c.*1885, became Ailsa

     Shipyard

     Davidson 1891
26. Girvan Jas Kirkwood

     McIntyre

     Ailsa Shipyard
27. Stranraer Dan Fyfe
28. Glenluce William Nicolson
29. Garlieston Hugh Jarret

     John McGreath

Bibliography

Anderson, J., *An Account of the Present State of the Hebrides and Western Coasts of Scotland* (Edinburgh, 1785)

Anon., *Campbeltown 1700–1950* (Campbeltown, 1950)

Anson, P., *Fishing Boats and Fisher Folk on the East Coast of Scotland* (London, 1931)

Idem., *Scots Fisherfolk* (Edinburgh, 1950)

Baker, W.A., *Sloops and Shallops* (Columbia, 1966)

Brabazon, W., *The Deep Sea and Coast Fisheries of Ireland with Suggestions for the Working of a Fishing Company* (Dublin, 1848)

Cameron, A.D., *Go Listen to the Crofters – The Napier Commission and Crofting a Century ago* (Stornoway, 1990)

de Caux, J.W., *The Herring and the Herring Fishery, with chapters on Fishes and Fishing, and our Sea Fisheries in the Future* (London, 1881)

Chapelle, H.I., 'Sources of Plans of British Fishing Boats' in *The Mariner's Mirror*, vol. XIX, no. 3 (1933)

Chatterton, E.K., *Fore & Aft Craft – the story of the fore & aft rig* (London, 1927)

Clarke, R., *The Longshoremen* (Newton Abbot, 1974)

Clowes, G.S. Laird, *Special Exhibition of British Fishing Boats: Illustrating the great variety of fishing boats in use, or recently in use, round the British Coasts – July 22nd – August 31st 1936* (London, 1936)

Coull, J.R., *The Sea Fisheries of Scotland* (Edinburgh, 1996)

Czerkawska, C.L., *Fisher-Folk of Carrick* (Glasgow, 1975)

Daniell, W. & R. Ayton, *A Voyage Round Great Britain*, 8 vols (London, 1814–1825)

Defoe, D., A *Tour through the whole Island of Great Britain (1725)*, 2 vols (London, 1927)

Dunlop, J., *The British Fisheries Society 1786–1893* (Edinburgh, 1978)

Fettler, J., *Scotiae Depicta* (London, 1804)

Finch, R., Sailing *Craft of the British Isles* (London, 1976)

Fraser, A., *Lochfyneside* (Edinburgh, 1971)

Garnett, T., *Observations on a Tour through the Highlands of Scotland*, 2 vols (London, 1811)

Graham, A. & Gordon, J., 'Old harbours in northern and western Scotland' in *Proceedings of the Society of Antiquarians of Scotland*, No. 117 (Edinburgh, 1997)

Grant, I.F., *Highland Folk Ways* (Edinburgh, 1995)

Gray, M., *The Fishing Industries of Scotland 1970–1914* (Oxford, 1978)

Hamilton, F., *Kipper House Tales – A Reminiscence of West Coast Life* (Ardrishaig, 1986)

Hawkins, L.W., *Early Motor Fishing Boats* (Norwich, 1984)

Hodgson, W.C., *The Herring and its Fishery* (London, 1957)

Holdsworth, E.W.H., *Deep-Sea Fishing and Fishing Boats* (London, 1874)

Idem., *The Sea Fisheries of Great Britain and Ireland* (London, 1883)

Johnson, S. & Boswell, J., *Journey to the Hebrides* (Edinburgh, 1996)

Knox, J., *A view of the British Empire, more especially Scotland, with some proposals for the Improvement of that country, the extension of the fisheries and the relief of the People* (London, 1784)

Idem., *Observations on the Northern Fisheries with a Discourse on the Expediency of Establishing Fishing Stations or Small Towns in the Highlands of Scotland and the Hebride Islands* (London, 1786)

Idem., *A Tour through the Highlands of Scotland and the Hebride Isles in 1786* (London, 1787)

Lethbridge, T.C., *Boats and Boatmen* (London, 1952)

MacAulay, J., *Birlinn: Longships of the Hebrides* (Stroud, 1996)

MacPolin, D., *The Drontheim – Forgotten Sailing Boat of the North Irish Coast* (Dublin, 1999)

Mannering, J. (ed.), *Chatham's Directory of Inshore Craft* (London, 1997)

March, E.J., *Sailing Drifters* (London, 1952)

Idem., *Inshore Craft of Britain*, 2 vols (Newton Abbot, 1970)

Martin, A., *The Ring-Net Fishermen* (Edinburgh, 1981)

Idem., 'The Mull of Kintyre Hand-line Fishery' in *Northern Studies – the Journal of the Scottish Society for Northern Studies*, vol 20, pp58–78 (1983)

Idem., *Fishing and Whaling* (Edinburgh, 1995)

Martin, M., *A Description of the Western Isles of Scotland circa 1695* (Edinburgh, 1994)

McCulloch, J., *The Highlands and Western Isles of Scotland*, 3 vols (London, 1824)

McKee, E., *Working Boats of Britain* (London, 1983)

Megaw, B. & E., 'Early Manx Fishing Craft' in *The Mariner's Mirror*, vol. XXVII, No. 2 (April 1941)

Mitchell, D., *Tarbert Past and Present* (Dumbarton, 1886)

Idem., *Tarbert in Picture and Story* (Falkirk, 1908)

Moore, Sir Alan, *Last days of mast and sail: an essay in nautical comparative anatomy* (Oxford, 1925)

Newte, T., *A Tour in England and Scotland in 1785 by an English Gentleman* (London, 1788)

Idem., *Prospects and Observations on a Tour in England & Scotland* (London, 1791)

Noble, A., *The Scottish Inshore Fishing Vessel – Design, Construction and Repair*, National Maritime Museum Monograph No. 31 (London, 1978)

Norton, M. (ed.), *Never Broken in a Sea, The Hebridean Workboats of Grimsay* (Kallin, 2000)

Norton, P., *The End of the Voyage* (London, 1954)

Pennant, T., *A Tour in Scotland*, 3rd edn (London, 1774)

Idem., *A Tour in Scotland 1769*, new edition (Edinburgh, 2000)

A Tour in Scotland and Voyage to the Hebrides, new edition (Edinburgh, 1998)

Simper, R., *Beach Boats of Britain* (Woodbridge, 1984)

Sinclair, J. (ed.), *Statistical Account of Scotland*, OSA, (Edinburgh, 1791–99)

Idem., New *Statistical Account of Scotland*, NSA (Edinburgh, 1845)

Slezer, J., *Theatrum Scotiae* (London, 1718)

Smylie, M., *Traditional Fishing Boats of Britain & Ireland* (Shrewsbury, 1999)

Idem., *Herring – A History of the Silver Darlings* (Stroud, 2004)

Stammers, M.K., 'Irish Sea Wherries, Schooners or Shallops' in Aled Eames *et al* (eds), *Maritime Wales*, No. 13 (1990)

Stewart, J., *Views of Campbeltown and Neighbourhood* (Edinburgh, 1835)

Stoddart, J., *Remarks on the local scenery and manners in Scotland during the years 1799 and 1800*, 2 vols) (London, 1801)

Tanner, M., *Scottish Fishing Boats*, Shire Album 326 (Princes Risborough, 1996)

Thomson, J., *Scottish Fisheries* (London, 1849)

White, E.W., *British Fishing-boats and Coastal Craft* (London, 1950)

Wilson, J., *A Voyage round the coasts of Scotland and the Isles*, 2 vols (Edinburgh, 1842)

Official Publications

Fishery Board Reports – abbreviated to F.B.R.

Herring Acts

Report by the Commissioners for the British Fisheries 1865, Parliamentary Papers 1866 [3596] vol. xvii

House of Commons Parliamentary Papers 1837–38, vol lii

Report of the Commissioners appointed to inquire into the Sea Fisheries of the United Kingdom, 1866 xvii–xviii

Report on the Loss of Life and Damage to Fishing Boats on the East Coast of Scotland by J. Washington, 1849

Manuscripts

Registers of Sea Fishing Boats (Scotland)

Customs House Letter Books

Other titles published by The History Press

Herring: A History of the Silver Darlings

MIKE SMYLIE

For over two millennia, herring has been commercially caught and its importance to the coastal peoples of Britain cannot be measured. At one point tens of thousands were involved in the catching, processing and sale of herring. Mike Smylie looks at the effects of the herring on the people who caught them, the unique ways of life, the superstition of the fisher folk, their boats and the communities who lived for the silver darlings.

978 0 7524 2988 5

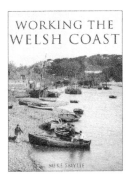

Working the Welsh Coast

MIKE SMYLIE

This well-researched and illustrated book looks at the types of vessels used along the Welsh coast for both fishing and coastal trade, from Tenby luggers, Mumbles oyster skiffs, Aberporth herring boats, nobbies and coracles to Welsh topsail schooners. Mike Smylie examines different sectors of the Welsh maritime industry and heritage, all in the narrative of a personal journey along the Welsh Coast from the river Severn to the Dee in 2003.

978 0 7524 3244 1

Fishing the European Coast

MIKE SMYLIE

The coastline of Europe has one of the most diverse collections of fishing boats to be found upon any of the continental coasts of the world. For the first time fisheries historian Mike Smylie has put together a collection of many of these craft through his own pen and ink drawings. From the great sailing boats of the northern herring fisheries to the small river canoes and beach-based sail and oar craft, this book catalogues a general crosssectional-record of European fishing boats of the last two centuries.

978 0 7524 4628 8

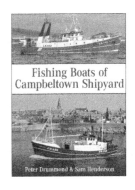

Fishing Boats of Campbeltown Shipyard

PETER DRUMMOND AND SAM HENDERSON

Campbeltown Shipyard was once part of a thriving Scottish industry. Today the empty buildings which comprised the shipyard betray no trace of the hive of activity which once existed there and produced some of the most successful fishing vessels ever built in Scotland, yet with former boats still turning impressive performances, the fishing industry will long remember the fishing boats of Campbeltown Shipyard.

978 0 7524 4765 0

If you are interested in purchasing other books published by The History Press, or in case you have difficulty finding any History Press books in your local bookshop, you can also place orders directly through our website
www.thehistorypress.co.uk

Printed in Great Britain
by Amazon